The Old Testament in Three Hours

The Old Testament in Three Hours

Richard J. Gill

Marshall Pickering is an Imprint of
HarperCollins*Religious*
part of HarperCollins*Publishers*
77–85 Fulham Palace Road, London W6 8JB
www.christian-publishing.com

First published in Great Britain in 2000 by Marshall Pickering

1 3 5 7 9 10 8 6 4 2

The scripture quotations contained herein are from the New
Revised Standard Version Bible, copyright 1989, by the
Division of Christian Education of the National Council of the
Churches of Christ in the U.S.A., and are used by permission.
All rights reserved.

A catalogue record for this book is available from the
British Library.

ISBN 0 551 03239 1

Printed and bound in Great Britain by
Caledonian International Book Manufacturing Ltd, Glasgow

Contents

Foreword
Rev Bernard Thorogood

Not many of us read carefully in the Old Testament, but those who do are transported into another world. It is a world of petty tribes and powerful military rulers, a world of many fears and hatreds. We read of local sanctuaries and idols and legends. And somewhere in it all we trace the story of one people and their journey of faith, from the earliest of records to the time of the empire of Alexander the Great.

Guides and interpreters are very important people. While there can be vigorous debate about the meaning of the inspiration of scripture, I think an even more vital discussion is about who the interpreters are. Who can illuminate those texts with clarity and sympathy and truth and human understanding? We have to confess that churches have often obscured rather than opened up scripture, giving fanciful interpretation to suit a particular theological viewpoint. And, like every preacher, I have to confess that I have sometimes strained a text to suit my own priorities.

How good it is to find in Richard Gill an interpreter who is not pleading a theological bias, nor is parading his scholarship, but is simply intent on seeing in the long story of the people of Israel a living message which touches us all. As a Christian minister, standing in the tradition of the Reformation, Richard Gill has come to value the Old Testament and make it his own; not to displace the New Testament but to provide the ground out of which the New was born. He tells the story. A whole range of human emotion and experience is here. Passion, betrayal, friendship, royal authority, fear, insurrection, ultimate trust and devotion – all are woven into these pictures of life under the hand of God.

And that is what is most valuable in this book for us, that it is about life in all its triumphs and disasters, but life that is not a mechanical process for conditioned robots: rather, a journey in faith and towards faith. The people of the Old Testament were very much aware of the great mystery of God and the majesty of God. We, who so readily sweep God off the human map, need this sense that God is the source and the end of all that lives. Thanks to interpreters who bring us such a key to an old lock.

Bernard Thorogood
Sydney, Australia
29 June 1999

Rev Bernard Thorogood is a former General Secretary of the United Reformed Church in the United Kingdom. He is an Australian citizen, serving a congregation of the Uniting Church of Australia. He served with the Council for World Mission in the Cook Islands for nearly twenty years before becoming its General Secretary. He has wide experience of ecumenical affairs in the UK and has worked with the World Council of Churches.

Introduction

I'm hopeless. Throw me a ball and I'll drop it. Throw me two, demand I juggle, and watch my horror. Expect me to cope with three and chaos descends. Yet this is exactly the challenge that the Old Testament expects of a reader.

It beckons us to read a story, but repeats itself like uncomfortable indigestion. The problems start within the first two chapters. Creation twice, with different orders and emphasis. Move through to Kings and Chronicles, and confusion reigns. Repetition is the culprit again. And why do the Psalmists paint pictures of God as a despotic ruler in one place but a gentle shepherd in another? Which is right? We must be certain of the nature of the One in whom our faith is to be placed. More confusion when turning from one book that narrates a particular point in history to the next, and the discovery is made that a total time shift has occurred and that we are in a totally different period.

The Old Testament beckons a second time with stories of people, people so remote in their living conditions that they can't relate to ours ... or can they? Different cultures, different ages, different modes of communication ... different everything. How can we recognize the nature of these people and their effect on community and national life? Sometimes these people behave in ways that are akin to bloodthirsty cruel warmongers – can these be the standards the Bible proclaims? Surely this makes the Old Testament outmoded?

Relevance is the third item to juggle with in the Old Testament. Not only are their times and lifestyles different to ours, but we are handling a span of history (1800 BC to 4 BC) so great as to make comparisons between the writings difficult, if not impossible. Can so many different ages speak to just one – ours? 'Yes' is the answer – and in ways which exceed all expectation.

How the Book was Born

A group of people had the courage to admit to me the fact that they didn't think they knew the story of the Old Testament as they should. This was despite the fact they had listened to sermons for many long years. They said they didn't know how the overall story unfolded, and challenged me to 'do something different'. Their experience matched others I'd shared with as a pastor during a quarter of a century. In trying to respond to the need, it was agreed that two things needed to be done.

The first was to tell the story in one sitting. Sceptics said it couldn't be done in three hours. The second need was to keep the story simple. An idea successfully used in the church study groups was comparing the characters and events in the Bible with counterparts recognizable in more recent history, or the modern world. This concept has been retained in these pages.

Personal Reflections

In preparing to 'do something different', and in the writing of this book, I have learned a lot. I do not regard myself as an academic, and this is not an academic presentation. It is, in essence, storytelling. Among my personal revelations is an understanding of why film scriptwriters change the order of some events when presenting a true story. In order to keep the storytelling flow, I discovered that sometimes part of a scene needs to be prepared in advance, even though it is – strictly speaking – out of order. I have tried to avoid this and to keep to historical accuracy. There are points, however, where the understanding of an event has needed this prior preparation. On other occasions the exact order of events cannot be determined with certainty.

The Old Testament is a series of writings which contain mystery: mystery through tales of the impossible (in human terms). For that reason, respect must always be given to the fact that there are many approaches to the Bible. Some who like the academic approach will accuse me of oversimplification, even trivialization. To that I respond 'guilty', yet justify myself in the struggle to keep the story easy reading for the sake of those to whom it is as yet new ground, or for those who find it confusing.

Some people come to the Bible expecting a literal interpretation of the Word of God. That need will be wholly supported in these pages. There will inevitably be points, however, at which I could be accused of taking a 'liberal' stance. It is difficult to do justice to both approaches, and I am bound to disappoint whichever approach is sought by an expectant readership. I'm that juggler, but now set on a tightrope – liable to fall either side of the rope. Help!

If the approach or line taken at any point is not your own, thank God for the ability to think it through. That is what this book is designed to do. Total agreement is never a prerequisite in life. If, in the end, people with opposite views can agree to differ but still share together the excitement of the unfolding story of God's developing relationship with humankind, we shall have discovered a unity with him and (through the Holy Spirit) with folk who think differently to ourselves.

This book, aiming at a three-hour read, can only be an introduction to the story of God and his people. The book is a taster of what happened. Only organized reading of the Bible itself can expose the true depths to which God has gone to reveal his love. His grace alone will lead us into fuller understanding of these centuries of exciting events.

One final part of the juggling act requires consideration. To whom is this book written? In part, for folk who have been in the Church for years but want to look afresh at the relevance of the Old Testament; in part, also for study groups. But, at all times, never forgetting people who need to start from scratch. I have to ask the patience of the first two groups if at times the Bible references or storyline state the obvious, for the sake of those making a first start into new areas of understanding.

All that now remains is to consider the best way to use this book – see the next section – and then to start. As the time clock used by British Telecom informs us, 'The time at the third stroke will be ...' Enjoy the next three hours!

Richard J. Gill
Lancaster, England
September, 1999

How to Use This Book

The structure aims to meet the needs of a range of readers, from those who are complete newcomers to the Old Testament through to organized Bible study groups. Priority consideration is given to enabling the story to flow along uninterrupted, covering the Old Testament in about three hours. Well ... give or take a bit!

| | | 0 | Target minutes used

Each chapter will begin with a guide to the three-hour target, a 180-minute counter, but don't get worried if your reading speed does not match that set by our publisher! At other points in the narrative another digital clock will appear: the date clock. This is present to help the reader set the events roughly into a time period.

| | | 0 | 0 | BC

In your reading you can achieve the story flow by ignoring everything apart from the first section ('Storyline') of each chapter. The 180-minute counter targets include only the storyline material. As you read you will occasionally encounter a 'flag':

Promise point

Ignore even these in your initial read! They will not be called for until Chapter 12, when reflection on the whole story begins. The 'flag' is intended to help quick identification when referring back to where some of God's promises fit into the story.

Having completed the whole Old Testament story in a straight read, return to Chapter 1 for a second reading, perhaps having a Bible atlas to hand. This time, handle the additional material, called

'Questionline'. The questions link back to the text of the chapter at points marked with a teacup symbol ☕. The questions allow the story to address modern life, or confront us with queries on what we have just read. More than one period of the Old Testament will occasionally ask a similar question to our modern era.

Once the art of reading the Old Testament is mastered, alongside an expectancy that it really does speak to our age, the less it will remain 'just history'. Far more questions of your own will reveal themselves than can be presented in these pages!

Mixed with the Questionline material are some Bible references for those who wish to read in more detail before addressing a question. The text of the Bible is rarely printed in this book. This is deliberate, for it gives every reader a choice as to which version of the Bible to use. We all have our favourites. Most references will either point to the relevant part of the story or to a passage which has a bearing upon the story. In view of the fact that questions invite a response about modern life, some Bible references contain New Testament material. Sometimes there will be no reference, leaving the reader in reflective mode.

Why use the ☕ teacup symbol? Relaxation is important in dealing with Questionline. The separation of Storyline and Questionline enables the book to be used for personal reading, personal study or in group studies. The sharing of thoughts, listening to others, is essential for spiritual development. However, not everyone likes organized study groups. If you are in that category, choose one other person in whom you have confidence and together work through the book. Either way, keep the tea flowing!

There is an old English saying, 'curiosity killed the cat'. As the story unfolds you may find yourself curious to read the actual Bible account. Don't kill the curiosity! Questionline has some Bible references, but particularly with those less familiar with the Old Testament in mind, a final section is offered called 'Bible Search'. In this will be found the source of a few of the stories mentioned in each chapter.

Again for those less familiar with the Bible, one final encouragement. Bibles are available in many formats, but two of significance. In one the text of a whole book is presented, broken up only by chapter and verse numbers. Others put in headings from time to time, much as this book aims to do, thus enabling easier identification of a particular story of interest.

The full list of Old Testament books is to be found on page 18 with an indication of their place in this book. Space has been left to add the page number in your own Bible, for ease of reference. The need to use an index is never a sign of ignorance, but of a student's determination to discover more about God.

In One Glance – HISTORY OF THE HEBREW PEOPLES

EVENT	DATE (BC) (approx)	BOOK IN WHICH RECORDED	WORLD CHANGES AND COMMENTS
Creation	Undated	Genesis	
The Flood	Undated	Genesis	
	2000		Mid Bronze Age
Abraham's migration	1650	Genesis	
			Decline of Babylonia
Isaac and Jacob	1600–1500	Genesis	
			Egypt strong
			Late Bronze Age
Joseph in Egypt	1500	Genesis	
	1400		Possible early partial Exodus
Exodus from Egypt	1280?	Exodus	
In the wilderness	13th century	Exodus	
			Iron Age
			Egypt weak, but revived
Arrival in Promised Land	1280+	Joshua	
Rule by Judges	1200–1020	Judges	
		Ruth ★	
	1100		Rising Philistine strength of hostility Egypt declining
Samuel the Priest	1035	1 Samuel	
Saul, first of the Kings	1020+	1 Samuel	
Reign of David	1004–961	2 Samuel	
		1 Chronicles	
Reign of Solomon	961–922	1 Kings 1–11	
		2 Chronicles 1–9	
Division of Kingdom into Israel (North) and Judah (South)	922	1 Kings 12	Egypt very weak but still able to mount raids in Palestine
	918	2 Kings 25	Assyrian revival
		2 Chronicles 10–36	
	750	Amos	
	750–737	Hosea	
	730–701	Micah	
		Isaiah 1–39	
Fall of Samaria and end of Northern Kingdom	722–1	2 Kings 18:9–12	
Southern Kingdom struggles on alone		Jonah ★	
	627	Zephaniah	Rise of Babylon
	626–580	Jeremiah	
Reform under Josiah and finding of Law Book	621	Deuteronomy	
Babylon captures Nineveh	612	Nahum	
	605	Fall of Assyria	

In One Glance – HISTORY OF THE HEBREW PEOPLES

Deportation 1 to Babylon	597	Habakkuk 2 Kings 24:10–17 and presupposed in Ezekiel	
Jerusalem falls, and the end of the Southern Kingdom	587	2 Kings 25, Jeremiah 52 Obadiah	
Deportation 2 to Babylon	587	Isaiah 40–55 Daniel ★	
Deportation 3	582	Lamentations	
	568		Nebuchadnezzar invades Egypt
	540		Rise of the Persian Empire
Babylon 'taken over' by Cyrus of Persia	539		
Cyrus permits return of the exiles	538	Ezra 1	
Homeward flow of exiles	537–390	Ezra/Nehemiah Jonah ● Isaiah 56–66	
	525		Egypt under Persian rule
Rebuilding of Jerusalem temple	520–515	Haggai Zechariah	
	500	Obadiah	
	490	Malachi Esther ★	
Nehemiah comes to Jerusalem	445	Nehemiah	
Ezra also arrives	428 or 398	Ezra/Nehemiah	
	400		Egyptian control dominates Judaea under Persian control
	4th century	Ruth ● Job	
Greek conquests of whole Persian Empire, including Palestine	332	Joel	
Greek persecution of Jews	168	Daniel ●	
	167		Jerusalem temple profaned
	164		temple rededicated
Jewish revolt against Greeks	150	Esther ●	
	63		Roman Empire takes Syria and Jerusalem
	4		Birth of Jesus Christ

Some books were written in one age (●), but the background of another historical period (★) has been used as a teaching aid.

The Old Testament Books – *WHERE THEY FIT INTO THE STORYLINE*

BOOK	CHAPTER	PAGE NUMBER IN MY OWN BIBLE
Genesis	1, 2	
Exodus	3	
Leviticus	3	
Numbers	3	
Deuteronomy	3	
Joshua	3, 4	
Judges	4	
Ruth	9	
1 and 2 Samuel	4, 5, 6, 7	
1 and 2 Kings	5, 6, 7	
1 and 2 Chronicles	5, 6, 7	
Ezra	8, 9	
Nehemiah	8, 9	
Esther	9, 10	
Job	1	
Psalms	5	
Proverbs	6	
Ecclesiastes	6	
Song of Solomon	6	
Isaiah	7, 8, 9	
Jeremiah	7, 8	
Lamentations	7	
Ezekiel	8	
Daniel	10	
Hosea	7	
Joel	9	
Amos	7	
Obadiah	8	
Jonah	9	
Micah	7	
Nahum	7	
Habakkuk	7	
Zephaniah	7	
Haggai	8	
Zechariah	8	
Malachi	8	
1 and 2 Maccabees	10	

Some books are dealt with only in passing reference.

Chapter 1

 **0** Target minutes used

Peoples of the Mist

> **Did You Cheat?**
> Eager to get into the book, you skipped the section 'How to Use This Book'? If so, your enthusiasm may have made you miss important ways to handle what follows!

Bible Account
Genesis chapters 1–11
Job (who, like Adam, found life went wrong)

STORYLINE
? **?** **?** **?** BC

Genesis, or 'Birth', or 'History of Origin'

Dare we start our Old Testament journey with a jest? The story that is about to unfold is a serious and sober one at times. But a home that has the missing element of laughter is an empty place. The Old Testament is far from being empty as the home of faith discovery, so perhaps a small smile is permitted.

'PRANCING NUDES PLAY HIDE AND SEEK IN GARDEN': banner headlines in the tabloid newspapers. Editors dispatch photographers, greedy to fill page three with graphic details. Will Adam and Eve also make the 'nine o'clock watershed' on TV? Scenes of apparent depravity move on – into stealing juicy apples from a tree, and without owner consent. 'Scrumping', it used to be called. Not very newsworthy. Painful too, climbing trees in your birthday suit. What *did* they think they were doing? Just what is in this opening scene of the Old Testament? The little jest must end. They were not actual apples in the story, either. Serious consideration now lies ahead.

Swirling mists, writhing. Chemistry-stinking odours, and lifeless fog. Then, like a breath of fresh spring air, a power surged through this formless mess. And from that power came creation, living creatures, animals, fish, trees, grasses – a whole unfolding panorama in perfection. ⚏ 1 They emerged into a created earth full of spine-tingling potential. As more power breathed itself into the clearing murk, out stepped humankind. Innocent, befuddled, confused ... how did their history develop? What is to unravel will be the picture through the eyes of one nation, Israel. But in these opening scenes we are seeing the 'people of the mists'. Perhaps Adam and Eve existed. Some would argue that they are symbolic of human creation. Here are scenes of humanity enjoying the fun of life, but then discovering that alongside fun comes responsibility. And within freedom comes the temptation to rebel.

Perhaps sympathy ought to be offered to the emerging couple when they start having a conversation with a snake. It's bad enough talking to yourself ... God enters these activities, and is disgruntled at what he sees. ⚏ 2 Their scrumping activities have been deemed disobedience, and the first picture of punishment follows. Humanity, like a child, had to learn a precise framework within which life shared with God would work. They were evicted from their home in that most idyllic of surroundings. ⚏ 3 Evicted to a future of indignity, pain, work and misery. Moralists might cry, 'Serves 'em right!' But they had received little previous verbal or written warnings about their conduct – employment practice demands that, at very least. Who portrayed this as part of a bright new world? The culmination of a week of *good* work by God? Yes: for even at a moment like this comes a touching picture of God's love for humankind. God provides both of them with suitable clothing for the new life which now lies ahead of them. There is no going back, they now have to make their own responsible way into the future.

When you have just been made homeless, to get your wife pregnant seems a daft thing to do. Just like a man. Adam managed it. Cain was born, with Abel to follow on.

Abel had a knack with sheep; Cain had green fingers. They represent a problem for their time – the traditional offerings to a god by nomadic peoples were animals. The new idea of staying in one place to grow a crop, and offer that to a god, created a whole new concept of acceptability (or not) by a deity. God asked Cain why he looked so disturbed, but to no avail. Cain lashed out, murdering his brother. The scenes of punishment recur, and a fresh picture of a human fugitive begins.

As the human population in the earth expanded, so did their ability for wickedness. The more God looked at this species within his creation, the less happy he became.

The Noah Saga

The picture changes. The date clock moves forward by an amount impossible to measure in any meaningful way. A little man with hammer and nails, knocking, sawing and waving a tarred brush with energetic enthusiasm. ☕ 4 He has built a boat. Boat? Half the length of the QEII, yet put together without the help of a shipyard. By some as yet unexplained piece of inbuilt migration (and uncharacteristic obedience), representatives of all animals and birds flock to him. The moment the builder puts his tool box away, they proceed up the gangplank to take up residence. Why? What God has seen in humankind has yet again made him disgruntled. ☕ 5 Violence and corruption everywhere. Disobedience (Adam and Eve) plus the ability to hurt each other (Cain and Abel) reveal the depravity of humanity. It has become so bad that God has reached a point of regretting even creating them. Punishment (or is it discipline?) needs to appear again. Cloudburst is a gross understatement for what is about to occur. Destruction, devastation and death is the new scene for all living things. For a long while, the idyllic world becomes entombed and silent in its watery grave.

Noah was deemed by God to be 'righteous' within a degraded society, a person living among society but isolated by adherence to a living faith. His handiwork, the Ark, became a means of salvation for his family, the animals, in fact everything entrusted to his responsible attitude towards life. Noah is a refreshing picture of human ability to be rational, thinking, planning and creative. Noah's witness to his community, prior to the deluge, had been like the words of many a preacher: ignored. Salvation was achieved through his rational commitment and trust in God, contrasting starkly with the rest of humanity, now swallowed up in watery devastation.

Oh what fun some academic commentators have had attempting to 'explain' the Flood. Caused, some say, by a geological fault that allowed salt water to flood the Black Sea, which until then had been a protected freshwater lake. Others blame a shift of plate tectonics within the earth's crust. The awesome power of nature to have done so in exactly this part of the earth was shown in the 1999 Turkish earthquake. Other observers throw in a meteorite collision with the earth, causing a swelling of water levels. All very interesting, and perhaps worth exploring. But conjectures are not the real point for anyone searching for a basic understanding of the Old Testament. Nor for those who through its pages seek to find faith in the God it portrays.

As with Adam and Eve, life does have fun, but that carries with it responsibility. Noah's community wanted the fun, but responsibility before God was forgotten. Yet even in this early point of the accounts, the word 'salvation' and the idea of God's sustaining mercy enter alongside pictures of punishment. The person of faith is seen supported by the God in whom that faith resides.

The presence of God overseeing the safety of human and animal representatives was followed by a promise, understood as renewed to all generations in the sign of the rainbow. 🖵 6 This everlasting covenant promised humanity the continuing presence of God, and the assurance that life will never again be fully extinguished by floodwaters. Meaningful words as the modern generation faces climatic change, ozone holes and El Niño devastation.

Promise point

When those tormenting floods had eventually departed, Noah's release back on to dry land was with thanksgiving that was genuine. He offered suitable religious sacrifice. ⏛ 7 Then he went out and got drunk. Oh bliss. Recognizable humanity!

The Tower of Babel

Population numbers expand, and buildings are the inevitable result. One, a skyscraper, was so high that it reached heaven. For modern construction methods this would demand steel girders, computer design techniques, reams of plastic sheeting to keep the workers dry and a criss-cross of scaffolding poles to meet the demands of safety at work. And that ignores the many cranes to lift heavy objects into place in the rising building.

None of this existed. They had no pre-prepared stone blocks to help. For them, humble handmade bricks, veined with iron, stuck together with tar in lieu of cement. But to make the project even larger, it contained not just this one massive undertaking, but the construction of a city to support the workers. Why, why, why? What was the point of it all?

The people depicted at this point of human development and throughout the whole Old Testament visualized the earth as flat, and above it a flat heaven. Heaven had seven 'floors', each grander than the last in the wonders of living conditions, each one being fit for better people, until in the highest heaven God is to be found – or, as they might have imagined it, 'gods' would live there. For in the times depicted, the concept within human imagination of one God was still awaited.

The structure of the whole was held in place by pillars at each corner of the flat earth, repeated on each floor of heaven above. The construction of the Tower of Babel is symbolic of humankind reaching by self-motivation for the heavens and all the perceived glories that would be found there. A yet more repellent trait to human nature is also presented: the desire to make a name for ourselves. The great nations of Assyria, Babylon, Persia and Rome, at different ages, all desired grand buildings to show a pride in their earthly achievements equal to that of any celestial god. The aristocracy of many nations have, even to fairly recent times, used building size as statements of status and wealth.

As the biblical people proceeded with their project, there was fear, the dread of human solidarity being undermined, expressed here as confused language. It could equally well have been creed, colour of skin, or the many other things that have divided the unity of humanity down the long years of its existence. They feared a language of confusion, and what a pun is attributed to the original language here! The language of Assyria and Babylonia is Akkadian. Babel (linked to Babylon) is a twist based on the Akkadian word Bab-ili or 'gate of God', and balal, which is from a Hebrew verb meaning 'to mix' or 'to confuse'. Lovely to see the Bible having a touch of humour, even at such a serious moment of human blunder.

Now there enters into the narrative the renewal of a dreaded scene: God is cross – again. How dare humankind try to assume for itself both elevated position and elevated opinion of capability, and draw around itself a protection of self-opinionated status! Punishment had to enter the scene. ☕ 8 Not this time through a flood. The treasured building project was abandoned, with the work force scattered in confusion.

The understanding of a Creator involved in human lives was real to the people portrayed in these opening chapters of the Bible. It must be retained and respected in our own times. These are people who stepped out of the time of creation mists into the reality of responsibility for their lives.

This chapter began with a light, even flippant, review of the creation stories. Deliberately, for this is how too many people approach it. We cannot, must not, end in the same way. If these were 'people of the mists', we need to remind ourselves that what is seen in mist is often distorted. Not this time. Not these stories.

These people present a power to portray the nature of humanity in potent realism, and in a way that challenges every individual, of every age. They were groping to understand responsibility. What we see is humanity trying to establish an unchallenged right to run life its own way. The whole Old Testament will trace, with vivid and living realism, the tensions and struggles created by such a reaction to responsibility, and to the God of creation power. What has already been seen is his loving providence at each step of mistake and failure.

The Torment of Job

The book of Job is a wonderful presentation of folklore in very dramatic form. The story has counterparts in the Far Eastern nations, in India, in Babylon and in Egypt. It has reflections of pessimism and scepticism that could reflect many parts of the history of God's people that is about to unfold.

Trying to date the writing is an impossible task. The prologue and introduction to Job have been seen to have the flavour of styles of life around 1600 BC – Abraham and the Patriarchs. It could also have been written any time between Solomon's reign and the exile (say, 960–587 BC), and scholars have argued that it depicts the background at differing points between Abraham and King David (1000 BC). Another approach is to date Job in the Persian period of history (450 BC) because of reference to 'the Satan', or just 'Satan'. The name Satan rarely appears in the Old Testament outside Job.

The opening part of the Genesis story immediately presents the reader with ideas of punishment for wrongdoing and banishment from life's rewarding potential. Misfortune is seen as the result of personal choice and sin. As a result, the 'serpent' which caused the fall of humankind has oft been likened to the nature of Satan. The same themes of punishment arise in Job, and because of the problems of dating the narrative, the writing is mentioned as early as possible in *The Old Testament in Three Hours*, leaving the reader to reflect upon its themes as the history of God's chosen people unfolds.

Job deals with the problem that misfortune must be as a result of personal sin. The Jews had no significant belief in life after death, only a shadow-style existence in an underworld called Sheol. So, as the history unfolds, and particularly presented in Job, reward and punishment must be handled in this life.

The story of Job is of three friends who visit him, later to be joined by a fourth. They try to explain suffering to him, but their answers don't seem to satisfy his situation, nor his suffering. The only answer is for him to wrestle with it himself.

In doing this, Job asks some searching and basic questions. Is God really 'Almighty'? Is God just? And: perhaps, just perhaps, humankind may be innocent. One solution to the problem of justice for the 'blameless and upright' (Job) in his life of piety is the intervention of a third party breaking into, and spoiling, the God–humankind relationship. That also is the warning of the Genesis serpent. The historical placing of Job is thus far less important than the relevance of the message it brings. He had to wrestle with an understanding of God, and that question will occur at frequent intervals through the Old Testament history.

Chapter 1 Questionline

⌨ 1 A God of creation is implied. What do we mean by this? Does it refer to God's original act of creation? When did creation cease?
Bible Notes ✎ Genesis chapters 1 and 2

⌨ 2, 5, 8 The opening scenes of Genesis are fundamental to our understanding of God–humankind relationships. What sort of God is being described at these points in our story? Is it right to assume God has 'moods', as we do? Can we be comfortable and worship a God like that? But could we be comfortable with a God who had no feelings, no responsiveness?
Bible Notes ✎ Genesis 3:1–15; 6:5; 11:1–9

⌨ 3 The snake story shows God as 'reactive' to what human beings are doing. Do we believe he responds and intervenes, and with punishment? Does a 'God of love' exist in this portrayal?
Bible Notes ✎ Genesis 3:17–19

⌨ 4 God chose Noah for this task. A good man, the Bible records.

Does this imply that God prejudges the final outcome of our lives? What happens if we improve after a bad start to life, or make a blunder, big or small, at some point? Remember, Noah did – or doesn't getting drunk count? When do our mistakes 'count' in the sight of God's anger?

Bible Notes ✎ *Genesis 6:9; 9:20–21*

✐ 6 Is there a hope in the rainbow sign that the ongoing cycle of crime and punishment could be broken? How could such a hope be made to represent itself in modern systems of civil and criminal justice?

Bible Notes ✎ *Genesis 9:12–17*

✐ 7 Noah did remember to offer thanks for his salvation. If this is a picture of a 'saving God', how do we face up to the context of violent destruction needed to achieve such a result?

Bible Notes ✎ *Genesis 8:20–22*

Chapter 1 Bible Search

The creation story	Genesis 1:1–2:4, Job 38:4–11
Adam and Eve	Genesis 3:1–24
Noah	Genesis 6:9–9:28
The Tower of Babel	Genesis 11:1–9
Job's suffering	Job 7:1–21
Job's restoration	Job 42:10–17

Theme Prayer

Father God, these scenes of confusion, mistakes and human activity within your creation speak not of far-off times, but of our age and our conditions. These pictures also contain messages of hope and scenes of salvation. Creator God, may these also be understood today. Amen.

Chapter 2

| 1 | 1 | Target minutes used

Family Life

Bible Account
Genesis chapters 12–50

STORYLINE

| 1 | 6 | 5 | 0 | BC

The telephone rings. At three in the morning it must mean some form of news. But what? Its tone shakes us from slumbering one moment to worried alertness the next. Such calls can change the course of life. God's 'calls' can also turn things upside down. 'Move!' came the command to Abram, 'and shift your family with you.' The phone may not have been invented then, but the message was crystal clear. And startling!

The scene has changed, from people in a mist to the lives of real people. Very real people. Some of the very special and treasured people in the early history of Israel. People who will display human weaknesses, and yet they could find God.

How good it is to feel family life around us, and to know it is secure and settled. Abram, alias Abraham, had taken over from his father as tribal chief, head of the clan or family. He was part of that lifestyle that had settled down. The family had made a secure niche for themselves in the town of Haran, until that call came to totally destroy a protected way of life.

Decisions to uproot and move home, for any head of family, are not easy. For Abraham obedience to God was a keynote lifestyle. 🏺 1 The extended family over which he exercised influence was immense. To be obedient to the call 'Move!' would be to devastate the lives of massive numbers of individuals – men, their women, children, aunts and aged grandfathers, along with as much of their homes and flocks as they could take with them. They all knew what obedience meant. Obedience to Abraham. This was to become a migration of people not dissimilar to modern equivalents caused by famine or war. The same dearth of food and water, the same squalor. The journey would eventually take his family into areas controlled by Egyptians, and through places akin to desert. When committed to such a journey there can be no turning back. You can never replant roots in life. They were gone the moment this vast family group started to move.

When famine strikes just as a potential new home is identified and settled, people are driven to the limit. It came, with devastating reality. Obedience faltered. Abraham, faced with leadership choices of responsibility on the one hand or a life dominated under Egyptian jurisdiction on the other, tried to protect his own life by lying, lying about the status of his lovely wife, Sarah, or Sarai. 'My sister,' he explained. Fancy doing such a thing in a nation noted for its stress on truthfulness! The deception initially worked, and brought riches pouring in his direction from eager and impressed Egyptians. It seems that a pretty woman could always turn men's knees to jelly and wallets to generosity. Yet truth has a habit of leaking out, and when that happened not only did the riches stop, but the whole family suffered. 🏺 2 Family, servants and animals were despatched to the vulnerability of desert dwellers. What value those ill-gotten riches now? Even if family suffering could be justified because of one person's deception, could the same be said of the Egyptian Pharaoh's household, suffering serious diseases at this time? God's man, Abraham, had a lot to answer for.

There was no way Abraham's extended family responsibilities could survive intact in the renewed nomadic life now thrust upon them. Separation was the chosen solution to the tension and disputes that undermined their developing lifestyle. Splinter groups went their own way from this time on. Yet when things went wrong for them,

Abraham had no hesitation in raising a mini army from among his own portion of the family to go and rescue the 'separatists', or to revive their fortunes. Tension through imprudent activities did not smash the ability to reconcile differences and quarrels, as one part of the family appeared to find more favourable places for their herds than others.

A new call from God comes into life. 'Do not be afraid, I am your shield; your reward shall be very great.' Do we have to revise the earlier picture of an angry God at this point? It encourages Abraham to open his heart, on a very personal level. Anyone who has been through the torture and burden of childlessness will feel for the man as he pours out his burden. So many in his extended family, but not one his personal heir. He had God's promise that his direct heirs would be as countless as the stars. Abraham believed. Briefly. But it didn't happen. Surrogacy was an option suggested by his wife, so that her husband could feel fulfilled. Lacking the variety of child-creating options of modern science, Abraham accepted the suggestion and 'knew' their Egyptian maidservant. What a delicate phrase some versions of the Bible use; and what success it brought. But sometimes the cost of success is heavier than failure, as Abraham was to discover.

Promise point

His display of impatience to await God's time for the first direct heir is understandable, and very human. But his action brought the danger of changing the essential relationship and trust between God and himself. It also changed the relationship with that servant in a way that turned the structure of his immediate household upside down. The servant, perhaps understandably, had an elevated sense of importance now that she had given a child, and a prized male child (Ishmael), to her master. She felt top of the pecking order, and there is no true wife, then or now, who would not feel deeply about her apparent loss of status. Keeping the peace between the two ladies was to be an important role for Abraham. What has to be asked is whether, morally or socially, Abraham had offended against the behaviour norm of his age by achieving a direct heir in this way. ☕ 3

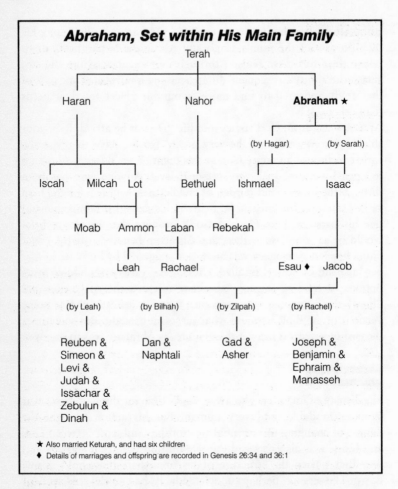

Abraham, Set within His Main Family

Terah

Haran — Nahor — **Abraham ★**

(by Hagar) — (by Sarah)

Iscah — Milcah — Lot — Bethuel — Ishmael — Isaac

Moab — Ammon — Laban — Rebekah

Leah — Rachael — Esau ♦ — Jacob

(by Leah) — (by Bilhah) — (by Zilpah) — (by Rachel)

(by Leah)	(by Bilhah)	(by Zilpah)	(by Rachel)
Reuben & Simeon & Levi & Judah & Issachar & Zebulun & Dinah	Dan & Naphtali	Gad & Asher	Joseph & Benjamin & Ephraim & Manasseh

★ Also married Keturah, and had six children
♦ Details of marriages and offspring are recorded in Genesis 26:34 and 36:1

Was there still present, between God and Abraham, any potential for future communication? Despite all the events, the answer must be a positive affirmation: *yes*! Abraham's dialogue with God produced a promise of a son, by his wife. But too much time had passed, and Abraham knew it was impossible. So did Sarah, and both shared laughs at the idea. At her age? The laughter had to be quickly stifled as they realized they were laughing at God's promise.

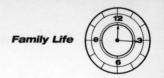

Promise point

Would this lack of trust now finally devastate the God–Abraham relationship? Or could the laughter possibly indicate that there existed a total confidence in the relationship on the part of Abraham?

Promise point

Confidence with God needed to come to the forefront of life when representations were needed on behalf of a degraded set of townspeople: a pleading with God, time and time again, for them to be spared rather than punished. Abraham begins a daring, yet apparently confident dialogue. ▱ 4 'Spare them if I can find among them just a few good ones,' he begins. But no matter how low Abraham set the numerical qualification for salvation, the townspeople's behaviour could not meet any criteria.

Should God now hide from his servant the terrible devastation that was to descend upon the towns, on Sodom and Gomorrah? The evidence implies that God could and did still love this man, and was prepared to show it in offered salvation to members of his family living close by those cities, which were noted focal points for male prostitution, homosexuality and similar activities.

This was a very salty area, and exactly what happened we cannot know for sure. If geographical evidence is taken into account, some clues exist. Fire from heaven. Tarnishing soot. Smoke that rose in a heavy black acrid stench – that is the general Bible picture. Petroleum seepage is known in the area, with attendant gases. Did lightning strike and create a devastating flashpoint? If so, we can appreciate how the explosion lifted soil and salt within the force of the fireball, destroyed everything, and everybody, with it. But explanations can never be satisfactory and are not appropriate. God had acted and that was, and must remain, the important point. What little endured after the event, in ruined state, was covered by displaced airborne salt. The acrid smell would have been revolting.

1 6 0 0 BC

Life sometimes surprises us by changes of pace. The scene moves
from devastation to emotion. Patience is at last rewarded, and the
true son Abraham's heart had longed for is born: Isaac. But what is
the nature of a God who, a few years later, calls for the child to be
sacrificed? Who is this God who demands that the father is the one
who must do it? Is God going to demand murder, under the guise of
sacrifice? ⌨ 5a

If there was ever a time for understanding and tolerance towards
human disobedience, surely this is it. Rebellion might not be a totally
unexpected response to such demands.

Yet from Abraham comes the quiet power of obedience. He is
ready with a faith that can march forward, matched by deed. He
prepares himself and his son. The tension rises as Abraham builds the
altar upon which he must lay the body of his son. The kindling has
been collected for the fire. Turning to the child, knife in hand, he
prepares to strike as the first act of sacrifice. In the nick of time, God
reveals provision for the child to be spared: a replacement sacrifice,
a ram caught in the thicket nearby, has already been provided. The
needs of the man and the needs of God's call to obedience were
reconciled at this climactic moment of history.

There is conflict in this man's character. High appreciation of him
here, yet possible earlier criticism of him for using a maidservant in
an act of faithlessness. Which was the real Abraham? In the period
between the two contrasts, he continued to be surrounded by a range
of concubines. One got promoted as wife when Sarah died. What is
going on in this man's life? What are the standards to be adopted by
a man expressing faith in God? What sort of witness was this? ⌨ 6

Living in a foreign land, as Abraham's current situation
demanded, with different traditions from those he had grown up
with, is a difficult challenge. Stick to your own traditions and you
separate yourself from community life around you. If you go along
with, or tolerate, customs that deny what you stand for, you
undermine your own credibility. Abraham decided that finding wives
for his children, and from their own homeland, would be the best
foundation upon which to build future obedience to God. It was a

demanding standard to set, and he needed to use a trusted servant to return home and find those suitable women.

Abraham died at a good old age. Yet the problems of infertility were to dog the family. God allowed himself to be entreated by Isaac on the topic. Rather than resorting to self-initiated solutions, Isaac left the matter to prayer alone. Waiting for an answer needed extended patience once again, but when it came, it came in abundance. Twins! Esau grew up to be a hunter; Jacob was the home-loving one, held precious by his mother Rebekah as a result. The tension rising between the two boys was more than just rivalry: it threatened the security of the whole family. Each parent developed a particular appreciation of just one twin. Divisive favouritism? ☕ 7

Have you written your Last Will and Testament yet? It is important. Saves a lot of tension and relieves many family misunderstandings when a death comes. Isaac knew he couldn't last for ever, and the version of a will in those days was the handing down of the father's blessing upon the elder son. What happened to this poor old man, blind and to a degree helpless, was nothing short of a disgrace within any family. While imminent death can bring out the most loving actions, too frequently it brings out the worst in families. It did here. The younger son, in collusion with his mother, disgracefully deceived the father, and cheated his brother of the blessing.

There was no way back. No undoing of the blessing, as there is no undoing of a will after death these days – at least not without resorting to expensive legal action, and that's an action that seldom solves family tensions. In the Bible story, the case of a lying and deceitful younger son created an inheritance from an unhappy and broken-hearted father. Esau had previously been forced by his brother to yield the birthright. Another view might argue that Esau himself had not taken its significance seriously in swapping it for a meal. Whichever was the case, the symbolic blessing is certainly now wrested from him. Every member of the family has been cheated of something: cheated of relationships, cheated of a happy confidence on passing into God's presence at death, cheated in love respect. Esau developed a depth of seething hate. Jacob fled, never to see his beloved mother again, fleeing to a different land and to distant sections of the now far-flung family links.

Stand back for a surprise. God did not turn his back on Jacob. He gave him promises of land and children. Jacob was not devoid of personal trust in God. Yet the irony of this comes later in life. Once contact had been made with his distant relatives, Jacob had the tables turned on him. He was to learn what it felt like to be tricked. He fell in love: love towards a most beautiful girl by the name of Rachel. The future looked as if it had a rosy hue. Don't we all feel like that when love is in the air? She had a sister, Leah – hardly a belle, to be frank about it. Even her name can take the unfortunate meaning of 'cow'! Seven long years he worked to earn the right to take the beauty as his wife.

There's a jest at modern weddings: on lifting the bride's veil the groom finds he has been married to the wrong woman. Our joke may be funny, but not for Jacob. The sisters really had been switched! How would you feel, waking up the next morning and discovering – ugh! The fact that he had to work seven more long years to earn the bride he really wanted seems poetic justice for his earlier unkind actions towards father and brother.

The problems in the family line concerning conception recur. It's the less-than-beautiful wife who becomes pregnant. And to rub salt into the wound it happens time and time and time again, leaving the loved and beautiful wife sidelined, barren and shamed. The fact that tensions arose between the women does not surprise, nor the fact that a servant maid was again resorted to as a surrogate to solve problems on behalf of the barren wife. What followed was a surfeit of children through more than one maidservant. Had this turned into undisciplined competition? Worse: almost without exception, the children were prized sons.

The Bible has a simplicity of phrase at this point: 'God remembered Rachel.' Joseph is born to the barren beauty. The unbounded joy will be understood by any mother who has had to wait for this moment. Don't forget Dad at this point in the narrative. This was not just another son – this was Rachel's fulfilment. And his.

Alongside family matters, the daily work performed by Jacob as

shepherd was causing delight to his father-in-law. But not all the close family shared their father's delight, particularly the sons. They still regarded Jacob as an outsider, and saw his work quality as having the potential of elbowing them aside. Jacob eventually had little option, rather than continue facing daily hostility, than to renew a travelling lifestyle. That in turn brought a new potential danger – of coming face to face with Esau once again.

He could only see that meeting in terms of confrontation. A dream the night before the encounter is no surprise. Or was it a dream – could every part of this encounter be reality? It projected Jacob wrestling with God. The outcome was injury to Jacob, but also blessing. His name became 'Israel', meaning 'struggler with God'. ♨ 5b What is being portrayed is a human being who could wrestle with the whole concept of God, could wrestle with people, and eventually come through with integrity. The meeting, when it came, turned into an enthusiastic reunion initiated by Esau that contained tears and a walking together. Reunion, and a reconciliation that could not have been anticipated.

Young Joseph grew and inherited the family prowess in shepherding. He inherited the love of his father, love well beyond that granted to the multiplicity of other sons. This favouritism we have seen before. Will families never learn? Yet the pattern of preferring the younger sons over the older ones will recur again in the Old Testament, as it occurs in the annals of other nations.

1 5 0 0 BC

Jacob's many sons attempted to exercise power. The scene again includes tricks. They must have had a good laugh on managing to sell Joseph, a bit of a dreamer they felt, into slavery, ridding themselves of him. Or so they thought. Was this act just family jealousy on account of Joseph being 'Daddy's favourite'? Or could it partly be attributed to the brothers' resentment of him being dressed in women's clothes – long, with sleeves (some say multicoloured)? Whatever was the cause of the 'disposal' of this family member by the brothers, a tale had to be concocted to account for his 'death'.

'Wild animals', they explained. It seems that the lessons about telling the truth were something else not taken on board within the family. But at least the story accounted for Joseph's absence. The cost of this deceitful project was the father's total and utter devastation.

Slavery was not unusual, as many were imported from Canaan, more normally as part of the spoils of war, but not wholly so. Joseph's slavery was about to turn back upon those brothers, as his life experiences now took him into Egypt. Here was a slave with ability, and as time passed his skills allowed him to rise from slave to employee, and from ordinary employee to a civil service-style responsibility and seniority. Along the career ladder, his abilities had been linked with the presence of his God within him. ⏧ 8

These were desperate times, and starvation was a frequent companion to nomadic people. His original family came into that broad category. In their hungry extremity, the family made risky journeys into Egypt for supplies. Unknowingly, they came before their once abandoned brother in his now elevated role. He had changed with the passing of years. They didn't know him. He recognized them. Time and again they came for help. Time and again they were not looking for or expecting their brother's presence. In the end he could hide his identity no longer. They had not deserved help, but they received it, plus a full, and again tearful, reconciliation.

Chapter 2 Questionline

⏧ 1 Around the world there is a process of re-examining 'family life' values and what they mean in the twenty-first century. The experience of Abraham is not uncommon when applying faith to life – God still makes claims upon us which may appear to conflict with common-sense care towards a family. How do we know what God is saying and discern the right way forward?
Bible Notes ✎ **Genesis 12:1–5**

⏧ 2 There is no family anywhere which has not experienced the trauma of coping with the effects of abusing truth. But what is truth?

How are we affected when telling the truth could undermine personal or family status and position? Are there not times when telling other than the truth could be an act intended of love? Is this what Abraham intended?

Bible Notes ✎ Genesis 12:10–13, 18, 19

☕ 3 The problem of procreation is a very real one for many. From some parts of the world we are hearing of falling male sperm counts, which could make things even worse. How, from within an understanding of God's guidance to humanity, do we reconcile the use of test tubes and artificial insemination on the one hand with millions of abortions on the other? Does the process of adoption address itself to this reconciliation? How do we view the modern problems over surrogacy in the light of Abraham's example?

Bible Notes ✎ Genesis 16:1–5

☕ 4 Keeping family life on an even keel is a problem for us all, and our prayer life is essential. But can we be over-confident with God? Too bold or argumentative in our petitions? Do we manage to express our inner self to God by just being polite, or using set books of prayers? If God is a 'parent' figure, does he mind us letting out our frustrations on him?

Bible Notes ✎ Genesis 18:16–33

☕ 5a, 5b We shall have to recognize many apparent 'faces' of God as we progress through the Old Testament. How many different ones have we seen so far, and can we reconcile them? What sort of picture of God can we honestly and accurately hand on to our families and the next generation? Are we 'strugglers' with understanding God?

Bible Notes ✎ Genesis 22:1–18; 32:22–8

☕ 6 What does this say about marriage as practised today? The acceptance of more than one bed partner does not seem to detract from God's appreciation of Abraham, nor of some other family leaders in these passages. Family security in the modern world is deemed to need the safety of the bond between one man and one woman. In the light of these Bible passages and evolving modern relationship patterns, can we justify the conventions of past generations being imposed on the future as the 'only way' for marriage? What do we really mean by 'marriage'?

Bible Notes ✎ *Genesis 25:5*

☕ 7 There are few parents who escape the accusation of 'favouritism'. How do we, can we, avoid it? Do these stories show that God favours some people more highly than others?

Bible Notes ✎ *Genesis 27:1–46*

☕ 8 How can a witness to God be part of parental example in the complex modern world? How can we witness to our faith while climbing a career structure more likely to be enhanced by sharing alcohol with 'the bosses' than sharing the Bible with them? By hiding our 'unfashionable' beliefs, would we enhance our chances of promotion, to the benefit of home and family life?

Bible Notes ✎ *Genesis 41:33–42*

Chapter 2 Bible Search

Abraham lies about his wife	Genesis 12:10–20
The Sodom and Gomorrah saga	Genesis 19:1–29
Isaac's blessing of Jacob in error	Genesis chapter 27
Jacob's dream at Bethel	Genesis 28:10–22
Jacob wrestles at Peniel	Genesis 32:22–32
Joseph is sold by his brothers	Genesis 37:12–36
Joseph's brothers get food from Egypt	Genesis chapter 42–46:7

Theme Prayer

God of Love, you have put within human life the ability to live together as man and wife, and to care for children within a family structure. We thank you for all forms of human companionship. Show to our age your ways of love that will continue to make life meaningful and give glory to you. Amen.

Chapter 3

[2] [5] Target minutes used

The Birth of Trade Unionism

Bible Account
Exodus
Leviticus
Numbers
Deuteronomy
Joshua

STORYLINE

[1] [2] [8] [0] BC

Slavery and Oppression

Israel (Jacob) and all his family settled in Egypt. The resounding crack of a whip was something feared by the people who settled there. The biblical account appears to focus on one family, in the main. They must be seen as symbolic of many families, groups or tribes. Here was mass migration at work. Their presence in Egypt was enforced to avoid starvation, but there was no such thing as a free handout from any Social Security office. ♨ 1 The glory days of

Joseph had passed into history. These were times of work, work, work to justify your presence in a foreign land. Not work in roles of personal choice: forced labour was the order of the day. Like it or lump it. These hordes of semi-nomadic peoples needed some feeding, and in coping with those needs the economic stability of Egypt could so easily have become undermined. If international aid agencies struggle with mass migration catastrophes today, with the aid of advanced communication networks, air transportation and the like, how terrible a responsibility had been thrust upon Egypt. Changes in their national government meant that the problem of food provision had come to the top of the political agenda. It had to be solved, and quickly. 'Earn your keep' policies were chosen as the only solution.

Birth control was another policy crying out to be rigidly enforced. The Hebrew people, like so many other migrant communities down the ages, were accused of breeding like rabbits. ☕ 2 The killing of all male children born to Hebrew families was the chosen solution. Barbaric to us, but what other options existed? No pill, no sheath, no advantages of modern medical knowledge were available to aid responsible citizenship among the migrants.

The work allocated under the 'Earn your keep' policy became harsh, building labour in the main. The size of the allocation increased on a daily basis, or so it seemed. It was a vicious circle. The workplace enemy of the Hebrew people was not just the whip to increase productivity, but the heat of the sun was also loaded upon their backs. They were not unused to it, but here no such thing as a siesta existed; not even the modern privilege of a tea break was granted to these workers. ☕ 3 Sweat poured from the bare, perspiring, sweaty, fly-attracting bodies of the brick-making task force. These were ruthless times. Work and terror were one and the same thing, from first light to the dying embers of the day. It seemed that the Egyptian appetite for building projects could not be satisfied. As more and more people flocked towards Egyptian security, so the food-growing programme became a priority, worrying local population and migrant worker alike.

A Life at Risk

As with all other parts of the human race, ingenuity entered the lives of the Hebrew slaves. For every oppressive rule imposed, an avoidance tactic was devised. They had no healthcare support services worth speaking of, no caring warm hospital for childbirth, just two cold uncomfortable stones for the mother-to-be to balance upon as a birth stool through the groaning hours of labour. Unknown to one mother, her child was destined to take a future role that would change all these circumstances. Relief, salvation from all this. But some people would later claim that the contribution created a change for the worse, not the better. Those changes were as yet light years away, beyond long tedious desert wanderings. What a good job parents cannot see the future tensions destined for their newly born children!

Moses was the child in question. The means of his escaping from the birth threats apportioned for male Hebrew children was devised by quick-thinking parents. A protective waterproof basket, to act as a cradle and hiding place, was placed in waterside reeds. That action created a new threat – the danger of being wrenched by the moving waters of the Nile river. The forces of fate were left to carry him into the unknown, no longer identified for sure as 'Hebrew', and so potentially safe from the penalty of death. Looking back on the event, later history could see the hand of God in this risky venture. It was to be a means of personal advancement for the precarious life of young Moses. Yet what a torture it must have been for a mother to risk the life of her precious baby.

The waters were to offer Moses into the care of the household of Pharaoh (the role title of king of Egypt) through the tenderness of one of his daughters. She found the basket with its inevitable hungry, and therefore noisy, inhabitant. The parental ruse was on the verge of failure, as the daughter of Pharaoh had suspicions. She found a nursemaid, perhaps unwittingly being tricked into using the child's own mother. How many more deceptions will these stories uncover? Despite that, instead of the crushing oppression he would have endured as a Hebrew, this child grew up in the palace, with status, and education. ☕ 4 He knew of his origins as the years went by, and his bond with the Hebrew people went beyond empathy. He cared,

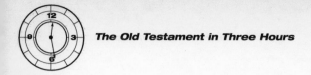

and it hurt. Hurt to watch what was happening from the ivory tower style of life in a palace.

The attempt to keep his feelings in check was important, but eventually impossible. Its release became his undoing, as year after year increasing burdens were placed upon the Hebrew people. Their treatment became intolerable, unreasonable, and eventually the matured Moses cracked. In an uncontrollable, untypical and impulsive action he lashed out, killing one Egyptian dispenser of torture. His semi-private allegiance was now in the public domain.

There was only one action left for him – run! He created a new life for himself in a far country, Midian. Humble circumstances by his old standards, working as a shepherd. But character-building. However, what he had as a lifestyle in Midian was still far superior to that which was the burden of his own people in Egypt. His inner concern remained deep, biting into his conscience in a manner not dissimilar to the originators of the trade union movement around the world in the face of industrialization. 🖵 5 Yet romance, marriage, children were all part of life for Moses. Life was great. At least, it would have been had the gnawing of concern for social justice not worked within him like incurable toothache.

Meeting with God

Religious confrontation comes when we least expect it. Curiosity killed the cat, so the old saying goes. A burning yet unconsumed bush stirred curiosity and became Moses' means of meeting with God. As he stepped towards it he felt a crushing sense of the presence of Yahweh, the name that would shortly emerge for God. His moment of commissioning to leadership of his oppressed people was upon him. And what a reluctant leader he was. He needed so much convincing, demanding evidence that the power of God was in and with him. Moses recognized that his future role was work given to him by 'the God of the fathers', knowing full well that when he got back to Egypt his countrymen would ask, 'Which god, what is his name?' To Moses would fall the combined task of identifying God to a people who had many gods, plus drawing them together into a united front. Union leader, theologian, priest and visionary. And if that were not enough, he would have to negotiate with Pharaoh for his people's physical release. Just as the birth of trade unionism contained input of religious zeal, so Moses would use the need for worship as a tool for negotiation. Separate tribes, families, trades, professions within the Hebrew people had to be given the vision of a life in a new Promised Land – a place that sounded like Utopia. But Moses' starting point was the very basic question, 'How?'

The Union Negotiator

His return to Egypt would be a high-risk strategy, in view of his previous brush with authority. Was he still a 'wanted' man? His brother Aaron joined him as spokesman in the negotiations. Pharaoh proved a very tricky person to deal with. 'Let my people go,' Moses pleaded with him. Promises to do so were reneged upon time and time again. Were the Hebrew people supposed to take Moses seriously when Pharaoh could treat him with such apparent disdain? ☟ 6 Harsh though life was, were the people willing to put in jeopardy what little they did have at the whim of a man like Moses? A dramatic and unexpected window of opportunity offered itself. Any trade union leader knows the importance of using chance circumstances to best advantage. Moses had learnt well.

Far away from the centre of this negotiation activity a series of natural events are thought, by some, to have played a pivotal role. Volcanic activity, either from a Mediterranean island or from the south of Egypt, unleashed itself with a fierce and fiery venom. Egyptian rivers, blocked by the falling ash, turned blood red as the new sediment was added. Frogs, gnats and flies stirred into untypical activity with the fallout impinging upon all human life. The welfare of livestock became virtually impossible. Fine dust created boils on man and beast alike. Thunder, hail and lightning created frightening havoc for the crops struggling to survive amid the rising layer of hostile dust. Food supplies were under a new and menacing threat. The option in the modern world, importing from alternative sources as a back-up to resources, hardly applied then. The future must have

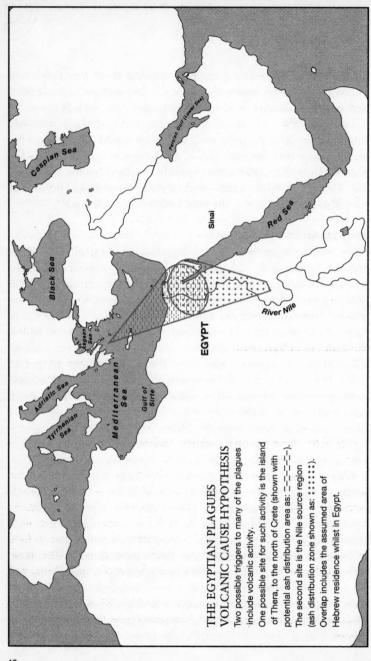

THE EGYPTIAN PLAGUES
VOLCANIC CAUSE HYPOTHESIS

Two possible triggers to many of the plagues
include volcanic activity.

One possible site for such activity is the island
of Thera, to the north of Crete (shown with
potential ash distribution area as: — · — · — · —).

The second site is the Nile source region
(ash distribution zone shown as: ¦ ¦ ¦ ¦ ¦ ¦).

Overlap includes the assumed area of
Hebrew residence whilst in Egypt.

seemed dire. What a time for a plague of locusts to arrive! A cloud of volcanic gas and dust created inexplicable darkness. Death came to members of families left exposed.

But we must pause. Temptations such as these towards 'explanations' for an interlinked series of surprising events may neatly fit the biblical portrayal. But never, ever, must the power of the hand of God alone to rescue the people of his choice be left aside. The name of God in Genesis 22:14 is Jehovah-Jireh, translated as 'The LORD[1] will provide'. The means of physical – and later spiritual – salvation is provided for a desperate people.

Under God-given circumstances, Moses pressed home his claims. Little wonder that with so much going on Pharaoh sometimes appears to have other things on his mind than just the plight of nomadic refugees. He could not focus his mood. 'Go,' he allows. 'No!' comes moments later. On some occasions Moses would underline to Pharaoh the picture of new dangers yet to come. On others he would take the negotiator's position of advantage, and leave him to be surprised.

It was the threat to human life that was to prove the straw that finally broke Pharaoh's determination. He was glad to be rid of these people. Glad to rid himself of the people he blamed for such an unexplained series of disasters. Glad to be rid of so many mouths to feed ... until the impact of the lost work force was realized. Lost potential for those essential building and repair programmes brought his old determination flooding back, and quickly.

God is at the heart of nature, ordering its activity to suit his purpose in the creation of a united people. When a barrier of water faced the newly released people, preventing their forward progress towards the Promised Land, they realized Pharaoh's armies were already behind them to restore them to their old servile status. God facilitated nature once again. An open path through the reed-embedded waters would sustain the escaping people, their flocks and

1 The word 'Lord' often appears in capitals in the Bible. Where 'LORD', or sometimes 'GOD', appears in this form the original implies the divine name, *Yahweh*.

light possessions. Not a heavy, laden and armed set of military fighters. The Egyptians sank out of sight in terrible circumstances. The slave people were truly free, at last!

Personal and National Responsibility

Freedom has both positive and negative aspects, as so many countries granted nationhood in modern history can bear testimony. Freedom is liberation. But within liberation, decision-taking becomes your own responsibility and burden. ⚏ 7 The Hebrew peoples were unused to this. Nor were they used to providing their own food resources in the way that they now would have to do. Many a children's outing away from parental control has been ruined by the demolition of an intended day's food provision in the first half hour of travel. Some of the same ideas occurred here, but the journey was to be longer than a day trip – forty years it turned out to be. They had forgotten how to practise many of the survival techniques their nomadic forefathers had used. As bellies emptied, so did the memory of Egyptian oppression and slavery. The solution to these tensions was one that humankind has always used: grumbling. 'The water is bitter' was the cry against liquid refreshment discovered on the journey.

Patience. Trust. These were the new political and spiritual buzzwords as the leadership of Moses moved into a different phase. An oasis was not far away, and containing an abundance of quality water. Those buzzwords had to surface again as they set out deeper into the wilderness journey. Threats towards Moses and Aaron came as the people recast their old Egyptian food poverty into distorted memory. Steak and chips it had not been, but one might have thought so from their attitudes under the new daily hand-to-mouth conditions of searching for sustenance during travel. Memory under pressure always twists fact.

Patience. Trust. Those words were heard again, and rewarded. Unknowingly the people were starting on a whole series of lessons that, over a whole generation, were designed to build them into a potential national unity, and to build a unique understanding of God.

The Miracles of God in the Wilderness Years
CONTRASTING PICTURES OF GOD FROM A SELECTION OF EVENTS

Exodus 15:23–5	Bitter water sweetened at Marah
Exodus 16:14–35	Manna, bread from heaven
Exodus 17:1–7	Water from the rock at Rephidim
Leviticus 10:1–3	Aaron's sons killed for making unholy fire
Numbers 11:1–3	God's anger sets fire to the camp at Taberah
Numbers 16:31–5	Korah, Dathan and Abiram revolt and die
Numbers 17:1-12	Aaron's rod comes into bud
Numbers 21:1–9	Lives saved by looking at a bronze serpent
Joshua 3:1–17	Jordan waters cease their flow

The leadership of Moses was to be questioned and tested time and time again. ⬚ 8 Was he a madman to take them along an apparent detour to the land promised as rich in fruit and honey, to take them into apparent unnecessary dangers as a result? These people were not stupid. They knew from nomadic memories that there were much shorter routes than the one chosen by Moses. One trade route would have covered the journey to Canaan in only four to five days. Their minds banished the greater physical dangers of the short cut. Their mouths uttered complaints about journey length. It was easy to blame Moses. It was just as easy to blame God – Yahweh, whom Moses was revealing to them. Who wants to concentrate on one God, no matter how unique, when he appears to permit or create difficulty at every step? The other gods seemed like the proverbial grass in the next field – always greener, always more sympathetic, always more active. Over and over again the people were tempted in matters of allegiance to God, and to his appointed leader.

Rules for Later Life
One of the essential lessons the people had to be taught was that of community living. It would need far more rules than wandering in a desert region. But they also had to learn not just relationships with

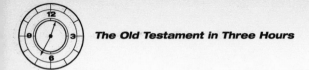

each other but, far more important, how to live with Yahweh. Here was the birth of the special covenant relationship with God.

Promise point

As the people stood and watched, Moses climbed a mountain to have direct dialogue with God. Not the most sensible moment to do it, for this was in the middle of the most ferocious thunderstorm imaginable, with hanging black clouds. What evolved were rules for life, that began with the revelatory identification, 'I am the Lord your God, who brought you out of the land of Egypt, out of the house of slavery.' The people were to have no other gods, not even images to help retain religious memory. A rest day was to be provided for worship. The importance of parental respect was taught. No murder, adultery, theft, telling lies about other people – all part of the new rules rolling out. Even a man passing an appreciative eye over a neighbour's wife seemed forbidden. What a testing set of guidelines! And how they were to be expanded in the coming years and centuries. Controls on employment practice, honour within the family, directions on interpersonal behaviour. Here is an important foundational moment in history as these ideas began to formulate.

Day by day Moses must have wanted to reach out for the resignation form as one tension piled upon another. Yet under his leadership the unique understanding of a supreme God was emerging. Painfully slowly. Yahweh was God, the leader and ruler of all the other minor gods worshipped by other nations and peoples. He was the Chairman of the Council of lesser gods. As an aid to learning and recollection they began to sing songs that would much later be recorded, not on CD or tape, but in the accuracy of folk music: the Psalms. That glorious picture of God presiding in a heavenly court comes through to us in the opening of Psalm 82. Deuteronomy 32:8 and 9, with Daniel chapter 7, from very different eras, take the same idea of subordinate deities all controlled by one co-ordinator or chairperson. The idea, germinating under the so-called freedoms in the desert, was to enter into history as a unique people knowing and serving one unique God. Only in the proper understanding of the principle of uniqueness could a 'relationship' be developed. A friendship can move forward with many people at one time, but a relationship has to be concentrated on one. Would it be built on the Genesis picture that there is someone over humanity who disciplines and is to be feared? If yes, then freedom from the Egyptian oppressor has been exchanged for oppression of a far more fearsome type. For God cannot be seen. The oppressors of Egypt could. The lessons these people had to grapple with had no easy comprehension or solution.

Life under an unseen God could not utilize work-avoidance techniques, so skilfully learned in Egypt to relieve some of the more oppressive burdens. The people were really in deep water. Moses often utilized his climbing skills in the desert mountain ranges. Not for sport, but to feel closer to God, for personal renewal, and to understand his message for the people. Somehow the mountain experience was a source of strength for this leader, to bring God's word to an ungracious and often deaf community.

Many of their rules and guidelines for life had striking resemblances to those in other great civilizations of the Middle East. But in these early stages of the desert journey, what was evolving was an understanding that their lives were part of a two-way covenant relationship. God serves those who first serve him. Every one of these guidelines affected the God–humankind relationship.

Promise point

The nearer they drew to the Promised Land, the more they encountered people who resented such a vast number of people passing through their sparsely grassed terrain. Hardly surprising that some unseemly activity took place, for the visiting herds with all their array of people would leave little or nothing that was palatable for the resident flocks. Here again, the delicate framework of human life support was threatened by these travelling Hebrews. Yet travel they must if they were to achieve the objectives placed upon them by God.

The travellers were learning what it was to be a people. What it was to be under the hand of God. What was meant by a discipline code. ⏛ 9 How to create styles of life appropriate to being a special, called and chosen people. They had to learn vital lessons about relationships. All these and many other lessons, had they been learned properly, would have stood them on firm foundations for hundreds of years to come. But these were human beings. They did not immediately understand more than a small percentage of this vast array of new knowledge. They did not always apply themselves to perfection. They slipped, and worshipped other gods. They became aggressors, thinking that this was reflecting the nature of God. It was; for the orders to do so came from God, and without any note of protest from him. Even when they had to be decisive, the buzzword about patience had to enter – somewhere. Their trust was tested. Their understanding of God needed to go forward in leaps and bounds, yet they had the same learning confusions that all generations have to share.

Mistakes, Penalties and Leadership

They made a real mess of things. Even Moses made mistakes. He was a man, not a demigod, and the reward of entering the Promised Land was refused to him. Death seemed cruelly timed within sight of the goal. He deserved his place in the presence of God, yet human justice would prefer a story that was rounded and completed in a picture of goal achievement, leading his people to triumph. Just as the people as a whole had to learn that punishment followed disobedience towards God, so too the life of Moses now had to submit. Even he had moments when he had broken away from God's will.

In this one life, in Moses, there resided the abilities of a union leader, plus a prophet, priest, judge and law-giver and, when things were difficult, intercessor between humanity and God. At different times he took the roles of victor, exile, fugitive, shepherd, guide, healer and miracle worker. Wow! A man of God, yet also with the abilities of a rebel. A unique man for a unique period of learning.

Joshua was Moses' nomination as successor. The Promised Land,

Canaan, would receive an invasion from these travelling people, who now wanted to take it as their own, but the process would not be without bloody resistance from the existing residents. Nor without discovering that some sections of the settled people were actually friendly! And not without the temptation of intermixing with the religious and social customs of the locals, particularly in the north. These were to prove troublesome temptations.

The entry into the new land began with an incident reminiscent of their departure from Egypt. Carrying the symbol of God's presence, the Ark of the Covenant, containing details of the covenant with God, so important during the travelling phase of national development, the people moved forward across the River Jordan, in full April flood. It blocked their path. Yet as they came to the barrier the waters held back, and they crossed safely on dry ground. What the story is trying to say is that the hand of God that had drawn them from the slavery of Egypt, and had led them through forty years of nomadic life, was assuredly with them now as they moved forward to take control of their Promised Land. As the priests stood in the centre of the dried riverbed, in the semi-tropical valley in harvest, God was recognized in miracle.

Worship in the Promised Land

Worship reinforced their feeling of the powerful presence of God as they arrived on the other side and began to renew statements of covenant. Here is a people intending commitment. They would need it, for as they moved forward the eyes of more than the local residents were upon them. This international trade route was vital to many other nations, as will be seen in the next chapter. They too were watching the expanding local population.

It is during this phase of settlement that the ability of God's people to crush others, using an apparently brutal and bloodbath style of cruelty, seems morally wrong and out of touch with a people expressing faith. No encounter with the book of Joshua can leave a reader with anything other than deep concern. It is unsatisfying to excuse this by saying that God's love in Christ had not yet been revealed. The book contains stories of many heroic actions, sometimes by larger-than-life characters. But even these cannot sweep away any of the horrors. Nothing can. These people were learning, step by step, learning more about God and his personal nature that must always be expressed in the lives of those committed to him. Modern warfare most certainly contains some terrible blunders, because errors will always creep in when pressures mount. They also occur in times of release from stress and restriction. ☕ 10 We have to balance just how much God was telling them to overcome local resistance and how much was human reaction to a difficult situation. We cannot judge after so many centuries. The real core message that comes out of the period of settlement is the constancy of God's presence and guidance, available to the people he had chosen as his own communicators of religious life.

Chapter 3 Questionline

How do we organize human life? The value of a human being is often measured by work status and/or earning capacity. How do we define 'work'? How do we responsibly measure financial rewards for work – by individual status, or by usefulness to the community as a whole? Has the modern world got the balance right?

☕ 1 There are moves in many parts of the modern world to restrict cash benefits from social funds in times of high unemployment. They sometimes come with demands for community work schemes. Does enforced community work demean the humanity of those out of work? Do they feel 'better' and feel useful? What is meant by 'the Protestant work ethic', and is it still relevant?
Bible Notes ✎ **Exodus 1:8–14**

☕ 2 Is it reasonable to expect people in difficult circumstances to deny themselves fulfilment through having children? When life is under threat there is an instinctive urge in nature to create large numbers of offspring to fulfil the demands of self-perpetuation. Are human beings exempt from this observed part of nature?
Bible Notes ✎ **Exodus 1:15–22**

🍵 3 The 'right' to make work more palatable seems enshrined in employment law in the developed world. What equal rights are fought for on behalf of those trying to eke out an existence in developing nations? Does the greater comfort of one set of workers adversely affect those who would love to emulate them?
Bible Notes ✎ *Exodus 5:5–21*

🍵 4 Our world seems riddled with examples of the contrast between those who have what they need for luxury and those who struggle for basic existence. Here is a picture showing that the contrast has been present since the earliest times. So would it be better if we accepted it as inevitable? What does such an approach say to the relief programmes of agencies world-wide?
Bible Notes ✎ *Exodus 2:9, 10*

🍵 5 The developing trade union movement has been filled with people of deep conscience. When is decisive action justified for the common good? What are reasonable bounds or limitations to decisive actions? When is the breaking of human law justified in achieving an objective? Can passive protest ever achieve a rebalancing of social justice?
Bible Notes ✎ *Exodus 2:23–3:1*

🍵 6 How is a religiously motivated person ever to be taken seriously in a world which relegates faith to a minor level of importance? Would a return to life-controlling fundamentalism be a way back to old standards? Can we ever hope to go back to old acceptance levels of faith as having a 'right' to address human life?
Bible Notes ✎ *Exodus 5:22–6:1*

🍵 7 One movement in modern working practice is that of 'power-sharing' between employer and employee. Worker buy-outs of companies, co-operative owning of companies, shares given to employees – all contribute to the blurring of old demarcation lines between those who give the orders at work and those who obey. Worker liberation brings the same responsibility to the modern worker as came to these people of old. But do we see these ideas as burden or liberation? Where are modern trends in employment practice taking us, and from what source of inspiration do we create future practice guidelines?

Bible Notes ✎ **Exodus 6:6–9; 16:2, 3**

☕ 8 Leadership by one person or one union is increasingly challenged in modern society. We demand democratic ways of working. What do we mean by democracy? How do we recognize it? How does it work within religious ideals, particularly alongside the picture revealed in our Old Testament reading thus far, of a God who dictates?

Bible Notes ✎ **Exodus 17:4–7**

If we all claim a say in every piece of decision-taking (one implication of democracy), can we still allow the guidance of God to over-rule? What place does God's rule take when we delegate our personal powers to human leaders, be they trade union leaders, politicians or employers?

☕ 9 Discipline is a strange word. An unfashionable word. Is it right to subject one person to the will of another by force? Is that what discipline really means? If we are held to God by discipline, what sort of relationship is it? But where would life be if there were no guidelines for responsible action towards each other, our community or our workplace?

Bible Notes ✎ **Exodus 20:2–17**

☕ 10 'Sorry' is reputed to be the most testing word in the dictionary. So hard to use. So effective when applied. In national, international, personal, workplace and other relationships, can the word be used without appearing weak? Is 'sorry' always an apology that indicates guilt or being in the wrong? Can a person of faith say 'sorry', implying fault, if they are following what they believe is God's will for their life or action?

For personal reflection

Chapter 3 Bible Search

Moses – birth and killing of an Egyptian	Exodus 2:1–15
Moses encounters the burning bush	Exodus 3:1–12
Pharaoh tries to recapture the departing Hebrews	Exodus 14:5–31
The Ten Commandments	Exodus 20:1-21; Deuteronomy 5:1–22
The Ark of the Covenant	Exodus 25:10–22; 37:1–9
Mistake over a golden calf	Exodus 32:1–35; Deuteronomy 9:6–29
Death of Moses	Exodus 32:48–52; 34:1–9

Theme Prayer

Loving Father, how can I organize my life? Conflicts of home responsibilities with work or care in my community, people who impact their life upon mine – and the other way round – how can I make sense of all these complexities? Guide me, so that my life may be used to your glory. Amen.

Chapter 4

How the West Was Won

Bible Account
Joshua
Judges
1 and 2 Samuel

STORYLINE

1 2 0 0 BC

What names we do give our children. Then we expect them to live with them! Allowing for translation from a different language and national environment, try these – Othniel, Ehud, Shamgar, Deborah, Gideon, Tola, Jair, Jephthah, Ibzan, Elon, Abdon and Samson. Who? Apart from the last-named, whose famous unsolicited haircut may ring a bell in the memory, and Gideon's adventures ridding the Israelite farmers of the nuisance of Midianite raiders on camels, possibly none stand out from the pages of history or the Bible with any degree of stature. Yet collectively they are an important body of people in the development of the Old Testament story.

Discovering the Promised Land

The books of Joshua and Judges tread on each other's toes, telling much the same story – the conquest of the Promised Land. With two such vastly different accounts, which is right? The book of Joshua has a narrative of whirlwind, violent entry westward into the country, from their position across the River Jordan, at the end of years of weary travel and hardship. Literally, a tale of 'how the west was won'. Judges, however, portrays a longer, more gradual progress, concentrating more on intertribal problems and marauders from outside – from Moab, Midian and, of course, those famous Philistines. A tale of perhaps a couple of hundred years of transition from a roaming rabble into a body of people capable of unity and nation-building. If the books of Joshua and Judges were just a historical record, we would have to point to the contrast in approaches and conclude one must be wrong. They are, in fact, both struggling to paint a colourful picture of something deeper than factual history. Both the tales are accurately told, affected in parts by oral tradition, even carrying quite reasonable exaggeration to make it memorable.

Both contrasting accounts contain bloody incidents, extending the discomfort that some Bible readers have with the now concluding accounts of nomadic years. What both accounts portray is a history of a people associated with the discovery of one, true God. No new discovery is ever understood in one lightning flash style of inspiration. ⬜ 1 Different aspects of understanding and behaviour are reflected in these accounts, which are to be read alongside each other, not in competition for accuracy.

A basic brutality to the age must not be dismissed. Such an attempt would denigrate the Bible. What lay ahead of those who wished to settle in a land of promise was battles, bloodbaths and killings. Yet these people's approach was not out of keeping with the norm of the time. Their actions would not have raised an eyebrow. We must always read the scriptures with appreciation of the age which they depict and the conditions they describe. What these accounts are trying to express is the feeling that God, discovered in nomadic times, was moving with them into a totally different phase of their practical and spiritual development. When an understanding of God stands still, so does spiritual development. When an understanding of God's relationship to real life stands still, morality declines and ethical standards lose their firm foundation. ☕ 2

Dismiss the idea of an empty geographical vacuum into which these nomadic people could move with ease. No Joshua story sticks in the memory quite like the battle for Jericho. The people of that city had made sure the gates were tightly closed just as soon as they heard of the advancing army led by Joshua. But no walls would stand against the will of God, who had promised in advance that the city would be taken by his people. As God's armed people encircled the city daily, the residents must have felt this a most peculiar 'attack' procedure. On the seventh day the priests blew their trumpets of rams' horns, as they had before. Forget the modern metal trumpet. These early versions made a most weird noise! On this final day the call came: 'Shout!' The walls proved their frailty, not their strength.

As this single story from among the many of the period demonstrates, this was most certainly a populated area. It was a place where intermarriage with the local population was an attractive temptation to weary wanderers at the end of a part of life that must have felt very isolated at times. But the rules for their special life, found in the desert years, forbade it.

Yet not all these local people were total 'foreigners'. There is a line of opinion that says that some were distant relatives, remnants of tribes that had not fled to Egypt many years before. Was a liaison with even them also forbidden? The rules for life started to demand a faithfulness from them that felt, at times, crushingly unfair. Even if some of them were direct relations, they had not been through the same 'God-discovery' experience that the wanderers had enjoyed. 'Enjoyed'? Can anyone 'enjoy' a life full of rules and regulations that even seemed to quash the spirit of freedom to enjoy that new life? What sort of religious life was this?

There are many Bible accounts that indicate that the experience of Egypt and the desert wanderings was an essential part of growing into an understanding of God and appreciation of obedience as 'separated' from all other peoples, even those who were, or may have been, related by blood. Many questions must have been in their minds. What was the nature of a God who demanded separateness? And why did he want it?

This was a key part of the fertile crescent. This was an area through which traders would regularly pass. This was a place envied and desired by far more than just the people who are the focal point of our current attention. The Hebrews were unwelcome, opposed and resented by many groups who depended upon the area's fragile status quo being maintained. But any people who want or need to be separate and distinctive within a community have to live with that.

If the tables are turned, and the viewpoint of those who lived or had stayed in the land is allowed priority, an understanding of the tensions is enriched. They had discovered very different religious and political allegiances. While any tentative family bonds which existed had been broken by the years and by experiences of life, there was still a fragile link back to early tribal days that were a common heritage. The attitude of the 'incomers' must have seemed to contain superiority, even priority of truth, in their claims to the land just on the say-so of their God. There remained a hurtful memory of being deserted by people who fled to Egypt, and in a time of great need. 🖵 3

Different races, peoples, tribes and faiths had merged in the area known to our travellers as their Promised Land. Circumstances and weather had repaired the original geographical and meteorological tensions that forced some into Egypt. While the exiles had been in Egypt, so many things had changed in this corner of the fertile crescent. Now the hordes of people re-entering the land were creating vast dangers to the established pastoral farming structure through widespread deforestation. The action was necessary to feed and house the now swollen joint population. Yet why should the resident population let these returning intruders create such havoc?

Looking at the story from the viewpoints of both residents and those arriving, it is not in the least surprising that what occurs is a tolerant reception in some places, but severe hostility in others. It is to be expected that we will find clashes of faith with secularism. How could the one be separated from the other? Faith is meant to work itself out in normal secular everyday life. Alternatively, if the secular cannot stand its ground within faith, then it must be resisted by people loyal to God. ☕ 4 These principles are worked out as a new story unfolds – the story of that group of folk whose names seemed so obscure – the judges.

New Forms of Leadership

The word 'judge' brings to the modern mind a colourfully gowned court president, probably in a wig, passing out wisdom and sentence upon those who need guidance and discipline in life. By virtue of their office they are frequently separated from the rest of the community. They have to be separated if their judgements are to be seen as totally unbiased and thus to be given respect in the tangles people sometimes weave in life. Their role, or calling, carries a degree of remoteness, separateness. ☕ 5

If this remoteness is what you carry over into the background and approach of this group of biblical judges, then forget it! Here are real 'characters' in the true sense of the phrase. Charismatic might be the right word, with a robust sense of human life. Instead of a formal view of their lifestyle, bring to mind the cowboys and Indians of American history. The Indians, in folklore, always raised up from among their tribe a charismatic as chief or leader, one who rose up to meet the crisis need of a particular moment for a particular tribe, occasionally uniting more than one tribe. Strong, with clarity of mind, being able to discern objectives and knowing right from wrong. Even, when need be, to initiate what we would think are bloodthirsty actions. But always with that objective in view which promoted and protected their own people.

In the wilderness wanderings there could only be one recognizable leader, taking the whole body of people in one direction. This concept was initially absorbed into the early stages of settled life as the people went westward, over the River Jordan and into this land of promise. This was a concept taken into the first campaign that gave them a firm foothold the other side of the River Jordan, from where they could lay siege to places like Jericho; taken also into the second campaign southwards, and into sometimes delicate alliances; and finally taken northwards into difficult hill country and onward into Galilee.

But once Moses' successor, Joshua, had died, and the people started to spread over an ever-increasing geographical area, the tried and tested single leadership system became impossible to maintain. Additionally, each area and tribe had different problems to contend with, each a different style of opposition to resist, each developing its own approach to settlement plans. Centralized or unified direction would have been a hindrance at this point in history. Centralization always needs a good communications system to ensure overall control. That had not yet been developed for a large geographical area. Even in Joshua's time, tribes had been known to act on their own initiative, rather than to a single command structure.

Yet the other side of the coin reveals honest dangers for physical survival. Smaller tribal units, separately administered, were more vulnerable than the single large mass of people had been. Worse: working out the meaning of germinal faith in one God could be easily undermined in unco-ordinated smaller groups. Worse still: diversity of approach made failure of the foundational Mosaic teachings a dangerous probability to be encountered. ☒ 6 The resultant ebb and flow in the quality of spirituality produced rebellion, often quickly cleansed by a return tide to the ways of God. They were struggling.

Agriculture was something they needed to brush up on quickly if hunger was to be kept under control. Why do the needs of our stomachs always impinge on life? Extended stops in the long years in the wilderness had given them opportunity to develop farming skills. The agricultural conditions of their newly acquired land were vastly different from those of Egypt, vastly different from the soil conditions of the nomadic days. The quick way to learn was to copy the locals. Locals who worshipped Baals – other gods, forbidden to God's people as one of the essential guidelines for life. The name Baal means 'lord' or even 'owner', and thus involvement in that form of worship acknowledged that people were neither the owners of their land nor in control of their life. These 'owner' gods could be female – Baalath or, by name, Ashtart. How great a contrast this was for the Hebrew people, for their God – Yahweh – was freely giving them use of this land of promise. The Ten Commandments, as they have become known to us, were their foundational guidelines for sharing life and land.

Tensions During Integration

Baal-worship had many essential ingredients designed to encourage fertility, both for the fields and for humanity. It incorporated such rituals as sacred prostitution, deemed a demonstration to the Baals of human good intent and purpose towards their 'owners'. What a marked contrast – disparity, even – between the stern approach of Israel's religion and this religious eroticism, which on the surface may have appeared to satisfy the need for human outward expressionism. It would be easy, but wrong, to equate Canaanite eroticism to modern interest in sex. The local farmers felt strongly that they could influence the rhythms of agriculture by copying what they felt were the sexual attributes of their Baals. The new arrivals needed the same levels of agricultural fertility to survive. The requirement to worship one God was starting to feel restrictive. It was one thing to note farming practices among their neighbours, but how far could they go in copycat practice and remain faithful to God? ⌨ 7 For farmers to ignore local agricultural practice with tried and tested customs would be similar to their modern equivalents ignoring the aid and skills of veterinary science. The new arrivals must have felt they were in a 'no-win' situation.

Why do we claim that compromise is a modern idea? They tried worshipping God and Baals at one and the same time. That helped their challenging tasks not one little bit. Confusion reigned! The two religious approaches were as different as chalk and cheese.

These difficulties in faith and practice came under the jurisdiction of the judges. Each tribe threw up its own respected charismatic champion, deliverer and arbitrator. They acted internally, for the tribe, and externally, to meet the challenge of invaders with designs on their settlement plans. Life had become a set of complex considerations for which no part or period of their past history had prepared them. The role of the judge had origins from appointments made by Moses. Judges could be priests, making the sanctuary a place where their judgements were proclaimed, and creating a link between secular administration and spiritual direction. Elders of cities could be judges, making their announcements in the gates of their town, but normally their role would not overlap with spiritual matters. Thus the role of the judge was a complex one, with different powers and responsibilities in each place.

1100 BC

Othniel, the first recorded judge, had to face up to the challenge of the people renouncing true faith and becoming subject to the rule of a foreign king. Ehud, the left-handed Benjaminite, had to rescue his people from eighteen years of oppression by the Moabites and their grossly overweight leader. Shamgar faced the might of the Philistines or 'sea people', while Deborah the prophetess urged her people to face the Canaanites. The better-known stories of Gideon are set within the struggles with the Midianites and the forays of Bedouins from across the Jordan, particularly at harvest time. Jephthah saved his people from the Moabites, but lost his virgin daughter in keeping a rash open-ended vow. What a mass of opponents were being thrown up, one after the other. Do we claim stress is a modern invention that affects life? Try theirs.

Some major judges, some minor, are in the list. They all make fascinating studies. The last on the list, Samson, or 'sun's man' as his name can mean, has tales recorded of tearing lions apart with his superhuman strength, dealing with riddles and setting light to the tails of foxes in his overall task of dealing with Philistine oppression. What a charismatic chap he must have been! But these stories are not recorded just for dramatic effect. What lies behind them is an evolving appreciation of theological understanding. When the people were faithful to God, they prospered. When they went down the path of following other gods, they discovered themselves to be weakened and no longer capable of standing up to challenges in life.

While some of these judges were appointed for specific times, tasks or tribes, there were times when their charismatic qualities became accepted over a wider tribal spectrum. Cross-tribe activity and leadership were providing the missing co-ordination. The place of faith applied to life was another unifying factor, and in religious life the town of Shiloh became important.

There had been an early settlement of Canaanite people in Shiloh, but it was the Israelites who were the first to build extensively. It became a place of religious pilgrimage, and its importance pivots on the period of the judges. We cannot tell exactly why Joshua had originally moved his headquarters to this low-level site surrounded by hills, north of Bethel. It had little or no previous religious significance; it was remote; it was unsuitable in military terms. The sacred Ark of the Covenant moved there, and this was what attracted the start of pilgrimage from all the tribes to the one site. 'The Sacred Ark', symbol of the presence of God, had taken on a very special place in religious life. The early references to it in the Old Testament imply a very simple wooden chest. But in other places it is described in terms of a golden shrine. Some references to it demonstrate that it was the portable throne for a God they could not see but did experience.

Shiloh, then, became a place where the huge annual festival could be held, drawing crowds of God's people from all tribes and places into a unity that was vitally important within this formative stage of the nation Israel. Unity through worship; unity based on faith. Whatever else went wrong in this age, here was a statement of national importance. 💬 8 But would the people apply the spiritual importance with so many other things crowding in on their daily lives?

Much later the tragic theft of the Ark from Shiloh, as part of a massive military victory by the Philistines, meant that the place ceased to have religious significance.

While religious worship could draw people together, a notable failure in unity occurred in military terms. The Valley of Jezreel stubbornly remained under Canaanite control, and only unity between the tribes could muster sufficient strength if the situation was to be redressed. Only half the tribes responded to the call for action. Later stigmas were attached to the unresponsive, for not coming to what was seen as God's call. It was evident that the need to remain one people was appreciated. Yet if they were to become one nation they could not keep going off at half-cock like this, even though a half-size army did win the battle. The cost in terms of disunity overrode any sense of physical victory.

Leadership and Unity

It needed a very special person to take this situation in hand and translate it into any semblance of destiny for the nation. A person with religious vision. An individual who could set aside personal opinion in favour of the common good. A special person of courage to take action that would create new and perhaps controversial styles of leadership in keeping with the demands perceived of a very different sort of future. A man with a strength of prayer who could intercede for the people before God, in the style of their former leader, Moses.

1 0 5 0 BC

That man was Samuel. He came from a fairly rich family within the tribe of Ephraim. His birth is a flashback to Genesis, and the tensions of conception. His mother, Hannah, on a pilgrimage to Shiloh offered a bargaining-style prayer to God. She promised that if she overcame her sterility and had a male child, he would be offered into the service of that shrine. She was blessed. She kept her promise. Samuel, while still young, came under the care of Eli the priest. What a task, to be tutor to a child destined to become judge, prophet and kingmaker. Did this little-known priest know the potential of his student? Spirituality in the nation was at a very low ebb, so much so that when the young Samuel heard the voice of God, even his tutor failed to realize the significance of what was happening. Eli's own family had such low spirituality that they were unfit to follow in their father's footsteps. The responsibility, by the call of God, was to be Samuel's alone.

One of the characteristics of Samuel was to call fearlessly for repentance from idolatry, so strongly that on one occasion God miraculously spared the people from the hands of a huge Philistine army. Samuel's standing grew, and he became so respected that his words were accepted throughout all the tribes on matters religious, on cult worship, on lifestyles and on personal, local and national issues of the day. To him fell the role of using oil for anointing, which he would consecrate for sacramental forms of worship, then in their embryo stages of development. It has to be admitted that some of these acts were confused at times with Canaanite religious practices, although not by Samuel himself. Samuel was no village clairvoyant, and everyone could see that. God had raised up an essential precursor of the great eighth-century prophets.

Leadership and Kingship

Honest difficulty has to be acknowledged at this point of the narrative. As in other parts of the Old Testament the stories are told more than once, from differing sources. Samuel's prime aim was to reunify the tribes into single leadership, yet he did not seek such a role for himself. What the general population had noted was that unity was achieved in other nations through the office of a king. In some of the records Samuel is seen opposing the idea, on the grounds that God alone is the ruler of his called and chosen people. From alternative sources his attitude seems more appreciative of the potential benefits to be gained. In either case, what develops is the concept that Samuel accepted and anointed the early kings, but not without demanding of them absolute obedience to God's law. 🖵 9

What a crushing responsibility this must have placed upon a holder of the office of king. Not just to keep God's law, and to have a lifestyle to prove it, but to know you had a man of Samuel's dominant power breathing down your neck at every step.

1 0 2 0 BC

The first choice for king was Saul, a man from a well-to-do family of the tribe of Benjamin. His home in Gibeah would have been of the traditional simplicity of its time, within a fortress-type village. Philistine pressures were great, and Shiloh had been smashed and its religious significance lost as surely as the Ark of the Covenant had been removed from the centrality of life for the people.

The crushing weight of Philistine dominance on life meant that weapons were forbidden to the Israelites. The spiritual role of Shiloh passed to a former centre of religious activity in Gilgal, and it was from here that Saul could establish his reign and plan tactics that

would confront these thorns in the flesh of God's nation.

The Philistines had an outpost at Gibeah. Saul attacked it, and to show defiance set up another seat of power in the place. That looked like a good start, yet the response was the mustering of the Philistine forces. Saul could do little else than muster all the troops available to him. His son, Jonathan, made the Philistines think deeply when he invaded another of their outposts. Some judgements of this action imply that it served only to precipitate even stronger retaliation. But eventual consolidated victory was Israel's, bringing absentee Israeli soldiers back to restore their allegiance to the king. The era of opportunity was upon the whole people: a time of revival for their spirits. The tide of national and military enthusiasm swept away more old opponents, the Amalekites and Ammonites. The lands, threatened by weak and disjointed tribal leadership, were now being made secure from north to south throughout this land of promise.

Yet even while this laudable phase of brightness applied to life, storm clouds lay on the horizon. This strong and able king had a series of thunderous clashes with the ageing but still strong spiritual powerhouse, Samuel. There was no way that the message of God would be silenced while this old man remained. Saul became impatient in one episode facing up to the Philistines. He failed to wait God's chosen time for progress, as defined in advance by Samuel. The delay had been defined so that proper religious sacrifice could be prepared and offered. Samuel's outburst upon Saul for his impatience incorporated the prediction of his fall from kingship. Strong stuff!

But the lesson had not been learned. Saul failed again when opposing the Amalekites. His order from God was for apparently ruthless extermination. Saul thought he knew better, and spared the Amalekite king, thus indicating a feeling of personal superiority to God. This outwardly kind action left God's people vulnerable, because a surviving Amalekite king could rally his troops afresh. ⏱ 10 Saul lost the support of Samuel but, more importantly, from then on he could not expect to find favour with God. A clash between matters temporal and spiritual was now inevitable, and Saul's whole personality changed into one punctuated by evil mood swings. All his outstanding and commanding achievements in securing unity and stability for the nation had been obscured by spiritual lapses.

Compassion towards Saul seemed demanded when he frequently admitted his faults. What he must have felt he received in response were refusals of mercy and forgiveness. The problem with his sin was in the core attitude of his heart and life towards self-sufficiency, instead of humility and God-dependence. Could it be that Saul felt that God was contained in a box – the Ark – and had not appreciated that God was at work in everything? Did he think that the loss of the Ark meant God was also lost? No, he could not have done. Yet his attitude to the responsibilities of kingship, instilled into him by Samuel, had changed dramatically.

Something better than this was needed if kingship was to stand the test of time. Had kingship led the people into a political confederation based on secularist principles? The idea that the head of state was doing the bidding and work of God had tremendous potential, but thus far it was an elusive potential.

Chapter 4 Questionline

For the most part, the questions arising from this chapter surround working out our faith in the midst of society. Some people seem to imply that the modern Church is lethargic and uninterested in anything other than what goes on inside their worship centres. So heavenly minded that they are no earthly good, so busy looking to personal faith that they lose touch with the 'soul of the community' around them. Could it be true?

♆ 1 Can any victory ever really be achieved through violence? What sort of God are we seeing now? Human life seems to be put at risk in achieving God's objectives.
Bible Notes ✎ **Joshua 8:1, 2**

♆ 2 The comments here are deliberately sweeping. So by what standards do we judge morality, ethics and behaviour, then and now? Can we adapt different moral standards to the varied ages as

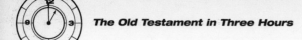

humankind progresses? If logic demands that we reply 'yes', then can we any more claim that the Ten Commandments stand for ever? But if we say 'no', are we happy to be bound by the rules given to an ancient group of nomads, and to impose them on the modern world?
Bible Notes ✎ **Joshua 6:1–5, 16–19; 24:14–18**

💻 3 It is always difficult to see history from more than our own vantage point. Assuming the original residents were related (which we don't know for sure), who was right here – those who returned to the land they had previously enjoyed, but abandoned in favour of what must have looked like easier options in Egypt, or those who had already been in residence within the Promised Land? These issues of land ownership are not so different from modern issues – the Falkland Islands, or flashpoints in Europe. How should we make such decisions/choices today? Is the basis fact, emotion or history, or some combination?
Bible Notes ✎ **Joshua 11:6–9**

💻 4 What is an appropriate form of resistance to the advance of secularism (life without reference to God) in the modern world?
Bible Notes ✎ **1 Peter 5:8, 9**

💻 5 In what ways are people of faith 'judges' of modern society? Is there a responsibility of separateness as part of our living faith?
Bible Notes ✎ **Ephesians 4:17–24**

💻 6 Our age is also full of diversity in approaches to life. There is a rising tide of recourse to counselling, new age solutions, alternative spiritualities, aromatherapy, to select just a few illustrations at random. How do we discern which ones support and develop faith, and which contribute to the potential of faith failure through undermining a trust in God, and God alone?
Bible Notes ✎ **Acts 17:16–32**

💻 7 This illustrates the classic tension of faith being developed in an ever-changing environment. What pressure do we see on our personal style of faith in a world that is surely changing much faster than theirs? What yardsticks could we use to ensure our faith remains true and undefiled? But what is the content of undefiled faith?

Bible Notes ◇ Judges 2:8-15

⌨ 8 Theirs was a period of wars and aggression, yet the elements of worship and faith remained of underlying importance. World wars had the same sense of uniting people in fairly modern history. Yet the wars against drug abuse, solvents, lawlessness and lost discipline do not unite people in anything like the same way, nor bring modern life to faith. What changes humanity during so-called peace so that we do not fight those things that undermine society?

Bible Notes ◇ Judges 21:10-19

⌨ 9 Would this be a reasonable demand on modern monarchs, presidents and prime ministers? Many inauguration or coronation ceremonies have words demanding it. So why does the population not demand the promises be carried through? Can heads of state really fulfil this role in any multi-faith society? Do people of faith (all faiths together) give help and aid to leaders in understanding a clear religious message?

Bible Notes ◇ 1 Samuel 11:12-15; 13:7-14; 15:24-9

⌨ 10 Does this imply that what is demanded of us is blind, unthinking obedience to God at all times as the only way of faith expression? How can we be certain that we really know what God is saying?

Chapter 4 Bible Search

Crossing into the Promised Land	Joshua 3:1–17
Jericho captured	Joshua 6:1–21
The Gideon stories	Joshua chapters 6–8
The Samson stories	Joshua chapters 13–16
A new, forgetful generation	Judges 2:10; 16–23
Samuel called by God	1 Samuel 3:1–4:1
The anointing of Saul	1 Samuel 9:27–10:8
	and chapters 17–27

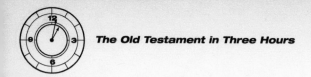
Theme Prayer

All-knowing God, help me to always look at news in my papers, magazines and television with the ability to see more than one point of view. If my church seems lethargic, challenge it – starting with me. When my government seems to fail to uphold standards, make me a praying person of faith, and so let me share in their burdens. In all these things make me obedient to your voice. Amen.

Chapter 5

6 3 Target minutes used

Rebel – with Good Cause?

Bible Account

1 and 2 Samuel

1 and 2 Kings

1 and 2 Chronicles

STORYLINE

Crash! The plate flies from the highchair, and hits the floor with a resounding thud. Dinner is splattered in decorative fashion on everything in sight. The tearful child has made a statement. The proffered portion of apricots with rice was certainly *not* what was appreciated. What has happened? Rebellion. To obtain a personal ambition or desire. As the parent clears the mess for the umpteenth time the idea of constructive rebellion is not uppermost in mind. Yet rebellion can be constructive, and because of that it is a reasonable human response under some circumstances.

Robin Hood, assuming he really existed, was a traditional romantic rebel in English history of the Middle Ages, a member of the nobility who lived the common life of the people, according to the time-honoured story. Hiding in Sherwood Forest, dressed in green, bow and arrow in hand, surrounded by a band of hard-done-by peasants, plus the chubby priest Friar Tuck and the ever-glamorous

Maid Marian, he had a very popular policy: 'Rob the rich and pay the poor.' His means of trapping and tricking the rich travellers through the forest to enable the policy to work may well be judged dubious from the point of view of modern ethics. But he was a rebel with a cause, a constructive rebel. Facing up to the challenges of his period, he sought to redress inequalities and social deprivation. Posh modern jargon – he'd have called it something far more basic, probably unprintable here. To change living conditions Robin Hood had to take risks, for the community and with his own life. He had a clear objective in view, and he stuck with it.

Two pictures. Rebellion for personal (childish) expression, and rebellion for constructive community purpose. The difference is important to the next phase in the Old Testament story, a phase that begins with rebellion, designed to bring the notion of kingship out of the doldrums into practical and inspirational purpose in the life of God's people.

1 0 0 0 BC

Samuel's Search for a King

Samuel had been drawn by God to meet the family of Jesse at Bethlehem. What a family – at least seven (perhaps eight) boys, and two girls. The day Samuel called and encouraged worship and sacrifice, the youngest lad, David, happened to be on sheep-caring duties. No matter how good his brothers may have been, it was upon this lad that God's attention focused, for here was the choice of future king, to succeed the sick and failed Saul. While the ideas of kingly succession had not yet been established, few could have expected God's choice to come from outside the existing royal family. Jesse's family didn't expect the choice to be upon one whom brother Eliab described as an 'impudent young rascal'! Nor could David, having been called and anointed to his future role, anticipate simply elbowing Saul aside from the throne he legitimately occupied. A complex set of issues lay before the shepherd lad.

The international situation stood in delicate balance at this moment, and clear-headed leadership was called for. ⬛ 1 It was not

just the Philistines who eyed the geographical area of Saul's rule with envy. Pressure was mounting on the whole of his people, north, south, east and west.

Some interwoven events now occurred. David became known in court circles. That came about through his musical abilities, so beloved by the gentry as they over-indulged their stomachs. Music has often soothed the troubled mind, and Saul appreciated the therapeutic value of it. David's gifts with lyre or harp and his growing connections at court linked him ever closer to the king's needs. At the same time, his youthful exuberance came to the attention of the military. Both these features were to play a part in helping the king, who by now was fast sliding into a state of periodic melancholy and depression. It was necessary to maintain a defensive army. Most families had young men conscripted, or volunteered. It remained a family responsibility to make sure their fighters were well shod, armed and fed.

Battle Lines are Drawn

It's not surprising, therefore, to find David among the army on a day when the taunting giant, a Philistine called Goliath, jeered loudly at them. The two armies stood facing each other. It was quite usual in those days to appoint a 'champion' to do some initial fighting. It had the potential to avoid a full-scale bloody battle. It also had an entertainment value to troops bored with the long period of stand-off between the two gathered armies. When this well-protected and well-equipped monster of a man came forward, it would be no surprise.

Nor was it a surprise that Saul's frightened troops were hesitant to volunteer one of their shorter members to respond. David was on the bread and cheese run from the family to his brothers, as he regularly was between shepherding duties. The insults hurled by Goliath were aimed at the king, his troops and, as a result, at the God they served. Week after week the diffident troops absorbed the insults. What unfolds underlines the fact that this crisis time was becoming a 'believer versus non-believer' battle just as much as it was a territorial one.

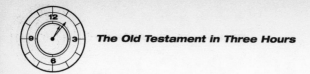

With the typical impudence of youth, David took his shepherd's sling and despatched a pebble at the man, just as he would have responded to a wild animal threatening his father's flock. The accuracy of the lad was perfection itself. With a thunderous crash the provoking giant was silenced for all time. The army of Israel was quick to press home their unexpected advantage, and the Philistines suffered nothing short of a rout. They were not used to that!

David's rise to fame was now unstoppable, even by a king who at first encouraged David with promotion but appears to have quickly realized that something was getting out of control. A pop song triggered a renewed deep depression in the life of Saul. The women sang, 'Saul has killed his thousands, and David his ten thousands.'

The alliance between the old man Samuel and the young man David plus the popular appeal of David's exploits were a package of events too much for the king's delicate state of mind. Lunging out with a spear, he attempted to pin David to the palace wall. Missed! But David's life within the court was now too dangerous. Yet, to rub salt into the poor king's wounds, his daughter Michal fell in love with David. The bride price set was one hundred Philistine male foreskins, a task judged just as impossible for a shepherd boy to achieve as it would be for him to afford the abnormally high sum needed to purchase the hand of a princess. Perhaps the king's thought was, 'Doing that'll kill him.' Wrong! As an idea it backfired badly. David produced the foreskins, became even more popular as a result, and won his bride amid ever increasing rapport with the people.

Worse was to come for Saul when family ceased to fully support him. The king's son, Jonathan, changed allegiance (or so it must have felt) and pleaded with his father for David, while Michal helped her husband escape from more regal persecution plans. David's escape was joined by the pathetic sight of the king in hot pursuit. Far from raising the majestic image of kingship, Saul was further humiliating the office by such actions. 💭 2a

Forest, Flight and Fear

A biblical version of Robin Hood was now inevitable, for David dared not return to court, nor could he be safe anywhere within the king's jurisdiction. He needed somewhere to rest, think and use one of the key abilities that were to shine from his future life: strategy. He took the counsel of Jonathan, with whom he had both a personal friendship and a formal covenant relationship that would later open the way to David's accession to the throne instead of Jonathan. David kept the support of his wife, plus the ongoing guidance of Samuel, who by now seemed to be the head of some form of theological school. David was in more than physical danger as he left the royal court. The potential existed for him to slide into national obscurity.

His chosen destination was the most improbable of places – among the Philistines. Madness, one would think. And, to be sure, he did pretend exactly that, to get himself out of one tight spot. His presence among the Philistines may have given him a measure of security against Saul, but he temporarily lived among people very suspicious of his every move. Yet these people, and probably only these people, were strong enough to offer him protection.

He could not stay there too long, and his flight – which was to make him a fugitive for many years – took him to the cave Adullam, probably capable of use as a stronghold for troops. It is here that the comparison with the tales of the English Robin Hood gain their most striking resemblance. David gathered round him a faithful band of peasants. Surprising people – discontents, debtors, those who were distressed with the way life was going. He also gathered members of his own family, including his parents. The fit members of the group were trained, made to feel respected, and turned into a strong mercenary force. He was at last surrounded by a group he could depend upon – a band who were destined to become a respected professional fighting force.

From one place to another David and his faithful band were pursued by the enraged and scheming king. David went on a personal excursion to another foreign territory, Moab, to hide his parents within their borders. With his current lifestyle, David could not offer them the love they deserved. 🖵 3 Probably only the king of Moab could offer realistic safety. Their king would respect David because of family links through his great-grandmother, Ruth, herself a

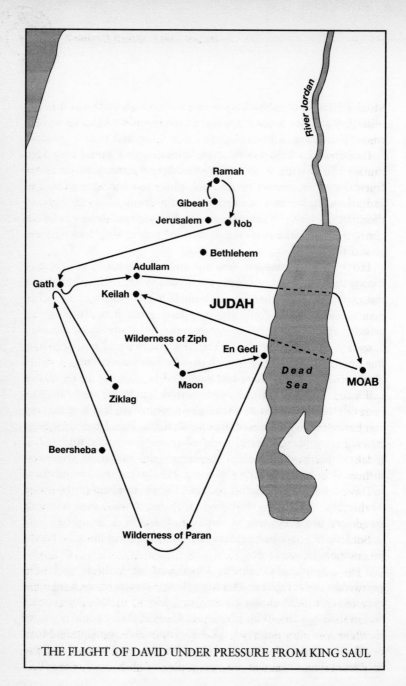

THE FLIGHT OF DAVID UNDER PRESSURE FROM KING SAUL

Moabitess. The Moabite king may also have given David military assistance, as the name of Ithmah the Moabite starts to appear among David's 'mighty men' from about this point.

David remained in the southern section of his future kingdom, gaining the respect of most of the people. Not all. News of his whereabouts was, from time to time, deliberately leaked to Saul, who had a good information network. Anyone who helped David risked their life. 🖳 4 This factor was among many that created the need for him to hide himself and his band way out in the desert. Yet even there he was not totally safe from pursuit.

David had his chances, within the inevitable skirmishes, to kill King Saul. That was a tempting path to power which David constantly and firmly resisted. Short cuts often lead to disaster rather than triumph, and this strategist knew that basic lesson. Despite David's ethical stance towards Saul, neither the king nor that element in society that leaked David's whereabouts gave up their persecution. The time to seek the protection of the Philistines had returned. Being outside Saul's territory he could not be hunted. For about one and a half years, David explained his activities to Achish, king of Gath (part of Philistia), in terms of raiding villages in Judah. The truth was that he and his men had been raiding, but the real target was Bedouin tribes, an action that made him very popular with the people of Judah! Good political strategy, perhaps, but can life be built on lies without penalty at a later date?

David had more than one band of faithful and trained supporters by this time, and slowly the whole of the southern section of Saul's kingdom could be regarded as 'loyal' to David.

But loyalty carried with it uncomfortable responsibilities, as David was to discover on both a personal level and as a leader of people. The Philistines decided to strike a renewed blow at Israel, and there are two views of how David handled the threat to his homeland. One view of the history shows David in support of the Philistines. The other shows him adopting a 'neutral' stance.

Whichever view one takes, there is no doubting that David was slowly re-equipping his loyal troops and ingratiating himself with the local leaders and community in the section of his homeland that had

been so helpful to him. He had built important alliances with neighbouring nations. The days of his fugitive Robin Hood-style existence were fast changing, and what emerges is a caring strategist, linked in daily life to the will of God.

The nature of the man is further illustrated by the fact that, on hearing of the death of Saul and Jonathan in battle, he set up formal mourning for both of them. Perhaps a less charitable leader might have ordered a party for the former! But David's honourable stature would permit nothing other than that which was right and respectful towards the office of king. 🍺 2b

It is at about this stage that the Bible again shows evidence of David as a musician with an ability to link words and music. A footnote on Psalms appears at the end of this chapter.

One King, Two Nations

After the proper period of mourning, David lost no time in marching on Hebron, and was immediately made king over Judah, the southern, helpful and loyal area. The ease by which he was crowned was evidence of the years of beneficial life his fugitive status had gained for him in terms of love and respect. Difficult phases of life are not unproductive. Rebellion against Saul had been constructive rebellion.

The northern part of Saul's domain suffered some serious infighting to determine a successor king to rule over it. This insecurity contrasted starkly with the consolidation David was noticeably achieving in Judah. Within the northern area, plot and counterplot continued to create an unsettled air to life, while the possibility of David also becoming their king gained credence. Eventually, the choice had to be made between members of the house of Saul and David's claim as son-in-law to Saul. It would be nice to say 'No contest!', but the truth is that the tension remained for some while. Eventually a group of representatives of Israel, the designation given to the northern tribes, came to David, having recognized three things. First, he was an Israelite; second, he was an able military man; and finally, he was willing to enter into a treaty or covenant agreement with them. David became king for the second time, now of Israel to add to the southern area known as Judah. A united monarchy was restored, and enriched, by a man close to God in ways Saul forgot.

What David had before him was the foundation of a 'Common Market' potential, two totally separate kingdoms, Israel in the north and Judah in the south, linked by one charismatic person: himself. The strategist ability of David now came fully to the forefront and, taking one task at a time and setting the minds of the people to it, trust in his prestige and charisma grew by leaps and bounds. The trust placed in him by other kings and nations was to be important for the future. Hiram, King of Tyre, donated cedar logs, plus the stonemasons and carpenters to begin building a palace suitable for a person of the status David now held in international affairs.

David moved his seat of power from Hebron to the neutral city of Jerusalem, or Jebus as it had been known in earlier times, a place acceptable and significant to both his kingdoms, a place of geographical and psychological strategy. From here David planned matters that would encourage the spiritual life of his nations, not just the administrative and secular community projects in life. Frequently plans were thwarted by diverting attention to battles. The Philistines in particular were watching his growing influence and control.

Despite these distractions, some semblance of the people being 'God's' did begin to re-emerge as a controlling factor, not just within the administration of justice and local politics, but as a significant factor in the whole of life.

Perhaps David's new palace was important on a personal level. He had his wives and concubines in Hebron, and as his status expanded so did his entourage. Now, in Jerusalem, he broadened the scope of wives and concubines, with a not unexpected expansion in numbers of children attributed to him. Why no critical word about his polygamy? Was he on such an upswing of adoration that he could get away with anything?

David, His Wives and Sons
WITH ALTERNATIVE NAMES IN BRACKETS

WIFE	SONS BY DAVID
Michal	
Abigail	Chileab (Daniel)*
Ahinoam	Amnon*
Maacah	Absalom*
Haggith	Adonijah*
Abital	Shephatiah*
Eglah	Ithream*
Bathsheba (Bathshua)	Shimea (Shammua) ●
	Shobab ●
	Nathan ●
	Solomon (Jedidiah) ●
Others	Ibhar ●
	Elishua (Elishama) ●
	Nogah ●
	Nepheg ●
	Japhia ●
	Elishama ●
	Beelida (Eliada) ●
	Eliphelet (Elpelet) ●
	*born at Hebron ● born at Jerusalem Bible sources: 1 Samuel 18:27; 25:42; 2 Samuel 3:2–5; 5:14; 1 Chronicles 3:1–9; 14:4–7

The troublesome Philistines eventually had to be dealt with by military intervention. The prized Ark of the Covenant was recovered and brought to Jerusalem. The joyous song and dance that led it back into the city was a natural expression of the feelings of the people.

Even David removed his kingly robes and replaced them with those of the priestly 'ephod' – a bit like a top-grade loin cloth.

What seems strange was David's treatment of the previously loyal and helpful nation of Moab. It was dealt with on the basis of exceptional harshness by David. Untypical: so some causal event must have occurred, but it is hard to ascertain what that might have been. When it comes to the Aramean peoples, the cause of conflict was clear – they took messengers of condolence as prisoners, and humiliated them. The Aramean states then became subject to David, but run by officials he based in Damascus.

In these ways, David's kingdom was extending its boundaries by leaps and bounds. His influence stretched from the boundary of Egypt across the vast tracts of land to the rivers and tributaries of the Euphrates. Some have attributed to David the accolade of being the most powerful ruler in the world at that point.

It all sounds so easy. In fact, it was hard work. David had both strengths and weaknesses to his character, but one thing shone out like a beacon. ☕ 5 His intention to stay close to the guidance of God. It was in the early days of ruling two kingdoms that David received God's promise through the prophet Nathan. As David had used a covenant relationship with his friend Jonathan, and again with the peoples of Israel as he became their king, now God was to make a covenant with him.

Promise point

Not for the first time, God had recognized in an individual particular qualities and abilities to listen to him. Relations between God and people and/or nations based upon the idea of a covenant or promise are spread throughout biblical history. The theme of trust between God and his people comes to the fore at special and particular moments of relationship development. Now, as David brought all the tribes together under a united monarchy, God made a new covenant with him. David would be the first of a line of family members to rule, so that the potential of an eternally secure throne would exist. The far-reaching implications of this cannot be overstated. ☕ 6 It

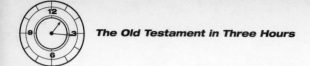

meant that the standards David set would now become a yardstick against which all future rulers would have their actions measured.

At last the settled people of God were being led in a positive way. At last they could not only establish 'their' land, but acquire control over much else beside. Their potential as a people of power was significant. The basis for the comparative ease lay not just with David, nor with the military skirmishes won by his troops, but in the international power struggle that must now become part of our essential background consideration of biblical history.

International Factors

For long centuries there had been power blocs in the Middle East. Egypt, Assyria, and Babylon all had their moments of strength and times of weakness. Sometimes weakness led to annihilation, sometimes to insignificance to rise afresh to later power, and at other times to absorption into a new facet of power-bloc structure. Geographically, little Israel and Judah sat in the major trade route that was an inviting path to armies eager to promote their own national interests. ☕ 7 Sometimes those armies would sweep up from Egypt in the south. Sometimes they would strike from the north as others wished to quell Egyptian advances. Time and time again, from this point onwards, we shall see the Promised Land and its God-directed peoples recording their history as if they were the centre of all that occurred in a troubled Middle Eastern political and military turmoil. That their presence contributed to the events cannot be denied. But often the major events which their annals portray had little to do with them, but a lot to do with power politics trampling through their land en route to dealing with larger fry than these minnow nations. It was all unfair on Israel and Judah, but how often life's pressures feel unfair.

Despite what is to come, the era of David's expansion must not be minimized. Yet it would be unfair not to take into account the fact that it occurred in a power vacuum, a period when no other power bloc was in ascendancy. For their one and only time in biblical history, God's people were the major Middle Eastern power bloc.

Under David they could enjoy it – while it lasted.

Feet of Clay?

It would also be easy to run away with the idea that David's life was perfection. His assimilation of Saul's concubines and wives and two extensions to the group in his own right showed his love of the fair sex. Not, it must be strongly underlined, different in action to many leaders of his time, to demonstrate status. He was human. Very human. His sideways glance one day from the palace roof locked on to the beautiful Bathsheba bathing. It must have left him wishing binoculars had been invented. She was not unmoved by the king's attentions and a child was on the way before they knew it. David arranged for her to become a widow in ways not in keeping with his normal creditable lifestyle. Bathsheba's husband, Uriah, was sent into a dangerous battle situation by David's express wish, with the inevitable result of his death. While David may not have done the killing himself, it brought more than discredit upon him. The displeasure of God was made known to him – not for adultery in isolation, but for taking another man's wife. David had clashed with two fundamental spiritual guidelines or commandments in one brief moment of passion: 'You shall not covet your neighbour's wife', plus 'You shall not commit adultery.' When David blundered, he made a good job of it! And his greatly extended family were to add to his personal discomfort and rebuke.

The pursuit of the national well-being meant that, despite his 'appreciation' of wives and children, he could be accused of neglecting them for more time than he should have done. As a man, if he could not keep control of his children, leaving them to incidents of feuding and inappropriate passions, what right did he have to lead a united monarchy? The separation between father and previously loved son, Absalom, was part of this situation, for Absalom felt so strongly that he led an uprising against his father. His strategy in attempting the throne of his father was carefully worked out. First came the undermining of confidence in the general population by exaggerating the worst excesses of his father's court. Building on that, he structured a clever coup d'état

by placing his loyal helpers in strategic places all over the land, with instructions to announce his accession to the throne at a predetermined day and time. David was so shocked that he felt he had no option other than that of protecting himself, and he left Jerusalem.

These events left in their wake the potential of creating tensions between Israel and Judah. Reconciliation was long and difficult but eventually came, and some lessons had been learned the hard way by all concerned. If personal charismatic control was not enough to hold together two men, the two nations that were David's prime responsibility and his wider empire also probably needed to be restructured for future robustness. 🖵 8

Other critics of this period of David's rule have said that he neglected to appreciate the workload of his population. Battles had sapped the national strength, and they had not been allowed for in the slowly growing need of what some feel was forced labour to achieve objectives. Here lay a source and germination of disaffection towards kingship. Another task placed extra tension upon the national energies.

9 6 1 BC

The taking of a census was a long and tedious task, but accurate data was as essential in those days as it is on today's Internet. The smooth flow of collecting the data was interrupted by natural and man-made difficulties: famine in one place, epidemics in others. While the census exercise could be understood in strengthening administration, it was judged to infringe religious principles, something that was to cause David to repent. As he grew older, the imprecise rules about succession began to raise family tensions again. He had many wives and almost twenty known sons, some of whom had been killed or died over the years. With many wives there were many 'first sons' to claim priority to the throne, plus many others both inside the family and outside who had military prowess, and who might well have felt themselves entitled to consideration.

David decreed, amid tensions, that Solomon should be the heir apparent, and after forty years as Judah's king and thirty-three years as king of Israel, David ended a glorious, rich and religious life. To his credit, he constantly consulted God as each step of strategy in progress for national life and consolidation needed to be considered. He was a man who knew how to repent when he made mistakes. ⌨ 9 His restoration of the Ark of the Covenant as a national religious symbol will for ever be held as a tribute to the finest king ever to rule God's people. He began life as a rebel. It was with good cause – the service of God, and the establishment of a co-ordinated and firmly established people, with a broader vision of their mission than just self-preservation.

The Psalms

It may seem to some archaic to maintain the appointment of a Poet Laureate in the United Kingdom. His role is to record current events and feelings in verse. The role reflects the fact that poetry can represent many features in life with a feeling that prose cannot. It can be very dramatic; it can record incidents in history; it can release romantic feelings. The list is endless. Poetry can interpret life, and can occur in the most surprising of people and places. Poetry is a free spirit. It need not rhyme, nor have prescribed metre. Many items regarded as prose can contain poetic rhythm.

The collection of items known to us as the Psalms contains many of these elements. They are diverse not just in style, but in the dates of composition. Many did find their origin in the times of David, and some at his personal hand – although even this can be disputed! It is less than fruitful to speculate as to which might be his. The gathering of such writings into collections probably began in the time of David, but were not finally brought into a full collection until well after the people had been in exile in Babylon. The collection reflects items handed down verbally for many centuries and additions made during subsequent periods through, and representing, the experiences of the exile.

These writings were both for personal use and for within worship. The collections brought liturgical purpose and structure. Not all of the Psalms speak of God in the same way: fear, love, respect, bold challenge, the ruler of other gods, the one supreme God, one to whom people turn when life goes upside down, a creator God.

☕ 10 Not all of the Psalms present a concerted picture of ethical behaviour or motives on the part of the poet or writer. The wide span of composers, composition dates and circumstances of the nation all mean that a single view cannot be expected to emerge. But this is a strength, not a weakness. It means that the modern reader can always find in the Psalms some representation of personal need. When our words to God seem dry and impossible to utter, our hearts can always find a ready common mind through the words penned by people of old, and thus we can release ourselves from arid spirituality. In the dominant praise, set within confession and a blatant search for the unexplainable in human experience, here are matters of the heart and soul.

Chapter 5 Questionline

In the main, the questions on this chapter are linked to leadership within the modern world.

☕ 1 In our day there have been lapses in the quality of leadership: moral lapses on national or personal levels, often carrying with them tragedy; lapses in military strategy programmes; lapses in honesty or truthfulness; lapses in so many ways. What are the basic qualities we expect from our leaders and those they call to work with them for the good of a nation or community?
Bible Notes ✎ *1 Samuel 4:1–8*

☕ 2a, 2b If Saul was demeaning the office of king at these points by his actions, could we also regard being a 'person of faith' as an office to which we are personally called by God? Can we humiliate God and our calling by our actions?
Bible Notes ✎ *1 Samuel 19:1–5*

☕ 3 Leadership skills demand that, in the midst of major episodes in life, there is no loss of touch with basic essentials like care of the vulnerable. Can modern leaders, with much larger populations under

their responsibility, really be expected to keep in touch with the minutiae of life?
Bible Notes ✎ 1 Samuel 22:3-5

4 This links to the previous question. Some people feel they help politicians and leaders keep abreast of the minutiae of life by making frequent representations about a whole range of topics. They are thus a good information network on matters which are concerning the population. But does this have the danger of distracting leaders from global issues?
Bible Notes ✎ 1 Samuel 22:11-19

5 On personal levels, it is good to see leaders of this status having two sides to their abilities. The modern media has a tendency to raise people up one moment, but smash their reputation at the first sign of weakness. Do people who express faith have a responsibility of pastoral care in moments of vilification, and how could it be expressed or made known to a leader in appropriate ways?
Bible Notes ✎ 2 Samuel 7:1-13

6 Do we see evidence that God continues to make promises, covenants, with people of stature today? How could 'stature' be defined or measured – is it just something that is a duty of those with national leadership responsibility?
Bible Notes ✎ 2 Samuel 7:14-17

The idea of a covenant relationship with God causes us to reflect on how the picture of God is changing. Do we still see the God feared in Genesis? How can we trace the changes, if in fact they exist? Does God change?

7 Modern history reflects changes in power blocs. The once proud British Empire is gone, along with the Russian grip in their part of the world. One could quote many examples of nations transferring to comparative obscurity. Peace treaties after wars so often realign national boundaries, only to have them break down at a later date.

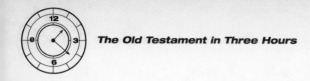

What strengths do we see in the current power blocs, and what makes for strength in the modern world? Is it financial power alone? Where is faith to be seen as part of the rise of a nation or power bloc?
Bible Notes ✎ *2 Samuel 10:1–14*

⛏ 8 The bigger the area of control, the more the problems of co-ordination. On what basis can the modern world reassess the usefulness and basis of power structures? NATO? Other defence organizations? Or the United Nations itself?
Bible Notes ✎ *2 Samuel 14:25–33*

⛏ 9 The ability for a person, and a nation, to repent is important within the whole development of the Old Testament. How is it reflected in international relationships today?
Bible Notes ✎ *2 Samuel 24:10–17; 1 Chronicles 21:7-1*

⛏ 10 It sounds a tall order to take pen and paper and search 150 Psalms for changing pictures of God. But as an exercise in drawing closer to an understanding of him it cannot be equalled.

General question on the life of Saul: a title often applied to Saul was 'the Lord's Anointed', meaning 'Messiah'. It seems that God had at first appointed him, and then rejected him by choosing another to take his place. Is this a picture of a God who forsakes his 'chosen' people? Could this change of heart be a facet of God that applies to modern life?

Chapter 5 Bible Search

Saul rejected by God	1 Samuel 15:10–26
David anointed as the next king	1 Samuel 16:1–13
David and Goliath	1 Samuel 17:1–50
Jonathan's promise of close support	1 Samuel 18:1–5; chapter 20
David's 'Robin Hood' period	1 Samuel chapters 21–4 and 26–31
David king of Judah	2 Samuel 2:1–7
David king of Israel	2 Samuel 5:1–15; 1 Chronicles 11:1–9; 14:1–7
David and the temple	1 Chronicles 22:2–12

Theme Prayer

Listening God, I cannot always agree with the leaders and rulers of my nation. Nor can I always concur with the actions of local leaders. Hear my prayer for them as they carry the burdens of office. Grant them strength and wisdom to fulfil their work for the benefit of all the population, without fear or favour. Guide them and use them, so that human life may be enriched. Amen.

Chapter 6

We Hate Taxation!

Bible Account
2 Samuel
1 Kings
1 and 2 Chronicles
Proverbs
Ecclesiastes
Song of Solomon

STORYLINE

There is no easy way to pay our taxes. Creating a national pot of gold is never a painless exercise for the citizens of any nation. Those in charge of the country's exchequer might not see it in terms of a pot, but to a taxpayer the payment always feels too much. An annual demand, weekly deductions from pay, monthly estimates of what will be due, even self-assessment – none of them are regarded with enthusiasm by any of us.

However, deep down inside us is a sneaking admission that all the things our taxes pay for have to be contributed by someone. But why can't it be someone else? Paying taxes, and contributing to national responsibilities, is something that is to take centre stage as the next phase of life unfolds for God's people. There are many views held on the impact and effectiveness of Solomon's reign which need to reflect themselves as we try to piece together the fragmented records of these years.

9 6 1 BC

David may well have made his wishes known about who should succeed him. His own anointing to be a future king was a surprise choice, so now also his nomination of Solomon was to create more than a bit of a stir. Under normal customs of succession it would have been Absalom, the illicit intruder into David's royal harem. But he had perished when his long hair became entangled in an oak tree as he rode away from battle. A self-created battle, it has to be acknowledged, to kill his own father and thus establish his own claim to supremacy. As he hung there, helpless, his life was brutally taken. ☕ 1a David's easy ability to restore Absalom's troops under his personal control afterwards was little comfort to the tragic grief that tore into the life of the father. So who now could take the throne with Absalom gone? Adonijah looked next in line, and he had certainly taken his opportunity to set up all the surrounding trappings of a royal prince. But his move to take over the throne contained both impatience and chosen supporters who were out of favour in the royal court. As a result he divided those around him, and only half gave him the support needed to be a realistic challenger for the throne, the others preferring the nomination of Solomon, the third in line.

Styles of Kingship

Having the ageing David's support brought success to Solomon, and his coronation was a splendid affair, with trumpets resounding all around as he entered the scene riding on the king's mule. But a question mark hung over him. He was a man with no military prowess. Even more important, where were the signs of divine appointment in the manner and style that Samuel had brought to his father as proof of royal nomination? Here was a man on the throne with few, if any, immediately apparent charismatic gifts, and little popular acclaim from the population. What particular abilities did this virtually unknown son have, apart from being the child of David's favourite wife, Bathsheba? That was not enough to make him acclaimed by anyone, and many of the elders of Israel and Judah stayed away from the ceremony.

Here was a king starting at rock bottom; but in many ways that is where his father began, and he managed to win the admiration of the population. Could Solomon repeat it? His first problem was clearly going to be brother Adonijah, who by that time had himself been crowned by supporters, although they promptly deserted him. It must have been a relief when Adonijah had the sense to swear allegiance to Solomon. That was not to be the end of the story, however. He eventually proved a threat to Solomon's position and he, along with a host of others, had to be firmly dealt with in ways that incorporated their death, or, in some kinder acts, house arrest. Here was the first demonstration of a significant difference in the style of the new king. David won people over. Solomon had removed his opponents by what can only be described as brutal force and barbarity. ☕ 1b In taking this line he set the seeds of discontent among the followers of those killed, notably those of the late Joab, a fearsome military leader of David's day. News of the death triggered revolts in Edom and elsewhere. Although David had taken Edom into his empire many years back, one of their young princes had fled to Egypt, from where he would re-emerge in maturity. Trouble ahead! But up in the north-eastern corner of David's empire another group was forming a breakaway section, led by Rezon, an outlaw-style character who would eventually make Damascus his seat of power. Now where was the inspiration from which they could have copied the 'outlaw' idea? The group was to be a continual 'thorn in the flesh' to Solomon.

Passivism in Leadership?

David's empire was so vast that it was inevitable that Solomon would need to be very astute if it was to hold together. One problem was that Solomon was still living on the prestige he inherited from his father. ☕ 2 As far as can be traced he never conducted any military campaign of significance. He had a different policy: defence. He

began by strengthening and creating additional fortifications around his core lands. From these he had flexibility to call upon troops at short notice if problems arose almost anywhere in his lands. From that action began to emerge an element to his rule that was to have profound effects for the whole of David's created empire.

The data collected at the end of his father's reign demanded consideration. It pointed to a whole host of opportunities for progress. What Solomon may have lacked in military experience was to be made up for in administrative prowess. Changes to local government controls impinged on life. Twelve districts were set up, with an official in charge of each. Far from the potential of weakening central government, the design of the districts cut across the original tribal boundaries established in the days of settlement in the Promised Land. One would have expected this to create riots, but that did not prove to be the case to any degree of significance. The new divisions stood the test of time. The courts were organized to put into effect political objectives, as the empire took on similar administrative patterns to those successfully adopted by Egypt and Mesopotamia. Here was a king aware of the world around him. Solomon was not unmindful of a promise he made with David to maintain religious life, and high on his agenda would be a project that eluded even his illustrious father. In the midst of it, all the royal bodyguard was merged with a section of the ordinary army. Does this indicate that Solomon now felt secure? Perhaps a better interpretation would be that the whole ethos of the kingdom was moving away from military dominance into evolving a new pattern of peacetime existence. ⚲ 3

Every administrative machine produces demands. In the modern world it may be for paperwork – everything in triplicate! No doubt they had their version of just that, but the impact under Solomon was significant in two particular areas, taxation and enforced work, as dual contributions to national life.

Building for God

The one thing that David had not achieved was the permanent building or place where God could 'live': the House of the Lord. The resources were capable of being brought together under Solomon, and the son set to work, virtually as first priority. A site was chosen near to the present Dome of the Rock. Trade agreements were entered into with Hiram, the King of Tyre, for the provision of construction materials – cedar and cypress woods. The workers of Tyre cut it, and it was shipped by rafting – locking together many tree trunks into a solid floating block. Having been brought along the Mediterranean to a suitable point they could be separated and taken inland in manageable loads to the chosen site in Jerusalem. The reciprocal part of the treaty was to provide Tyre with food. Keeping this part of a Common Market-style agreement was to open a massive rift in the coffers of Solomon's nation. The food requirements went on for years, plus covering the services of the tradesmen brought in to oversee the project, and the needs of food for his own people. It left Solomon in danger of a precarious financial situation. He eventually had to resort to mortgaging cities in Galilee, but that in turn only led to greater repayment problems.

The finishing of the temple was the excuse for a massive party. Sacrifices, celebration, pomp and ceremony, and the placing of the Ark of the Covenant in what was to become the most holy part of the new place of worship. Not long after his reign, that pivotal symbol of Jewish worship strangely vanished without trace. Despite searches and rumours of its presence in places like Scotland and Ethiopia, it has never been seen again to this day.

It is both interesting and significant that the multifaceted role of kingship was demonstrated through Solomon acting as priest for at least part of the opening dedication ceremony. ⛏ 4 Respect must be given to the man for his religious ideals exemplified by this glorious and prestigious project. His recorded dreams surrounded matters of worship, and his own ceremonial sacrifices were an important matter in making Solomon the man he was. From the start of his reign, his encounter with God, pleading for the ability to know the difference between good and evil, had been influential in him gaining the reputation for wisdom. He certainly inherited from his father the ability to collect songs and proverbs. There are almost as many works outside the Bible attributed to his collection as there are in it.

He loved word play, riddles and jokes which he reputedly exchanged with such people as the Queen of Sheba. But the assumption of wisdom needs to be shown in his rule, not his joke book. There are darker sides to his life.

If one building project seemed to be placing burdens upon the national exchequer, the pressures are underlined when other simultaneous projects are appreciated. Plus more to follow. The progress of those defence sites around the empire continued at quite a pace. They were each of quite significant size – perhaps capable of holding around three hundred troops and their horses plus supporting personnel. Solomon had introduced chariots to his troops for the first time – a novel idea again borrowed from other nations which had used them for long years. Now his own military machine was being modernized. These created a demand for yet more military space, even in a time of defence-only strategy. Development of the palace in Jerusalem, the building of an armoury, and a multitude of places of worship to cover the needs of Solomon's many foreign wives (a topic we shall return to shortly) continued the list of building works. Industry was something fairly new, and the scourge of modern life – an industrial estate – was developed for iron and copper smelting at Ezion-Geber. That was probably to become the biggest in the Middle East at the time, although a number of them would be needed around his empire. Solomon was stretching his exchequer more and more. He was also stretching his sphere of influence through another state enterprise – that of ship-building. 🖵 5 There is evidence that his fleet traded as far away as India, taking his name and reputation with it.

Servitude and Bondage

A money-saving idea he was to pick up from his father's time was that of using forced labour. One record of this action says that all the indigenous people were used. Another says it was 'all Israel'. The successor generation of the former slaves in Egypt knew what that lifestyle was like, but were now creating their own people of burden. In fairness to him and his father, it should be noted that it was a well-established practice of their age to use people like this, but could their memories not have warned them against it? Could they not have avoided this sort of 'earn your keep' returning as a life-controlling policy?

Slavery of all those previously captured in war was widespread during the time of Solomon – they were virtually state slaves. But there are indications that it went beyond the spoils of war to some of the original, less warlike inhabitants of the Promised Land. These all contributed through their free labour to the economy of the age. They, in turn, were joined in forced labour groups by the inhabitants of lands taken into the empire in stages during David's rule and developed under Solomon. These were 'worker slaves', to be seen as separate from the 'temple slaves' whose role was no less work but assigned to the priests, to serve their needs and permit worship to go forward. But the crunch question that has to be raised is: was all this massive work force really 'free' labour? The provision of their food alone was a burden upon the state economy, just as it had been for Egypt coping with the inflow of Hebrew people years before. Few farmers or even rich households could afford a slave in those times, so one has to assume the total effect, even after the physical contributions they made, was more likely to become a net drain on national resources. More problems to be faced by the man of wisdom.

Wives and Worship

Solomon was gradually ensuring the strength of his rule with alliances with Egypt, Tyre, Sidon and others. These alliances could be bonded by the acceptance of goodwill gifts, often of foreign wives, into his palace. The building of places of worship to enable the wives to maintain obedience to their gods was to become an Achilles' heel for Solomon. The size of the problem can be judged by the fact that the number of royal wives came to seven hundred, plus around three hundred concubines. The number of foreign royal wives he could acquire through alliances is uncounted, but the practice indicated the weakness of the dynasties of those nations. Whoever would have thought that once-proud Egypt would allow the ruler of former mini-state Israel to take one of their princesses, and to give him land as a dowry! Solomon was, despite the alliances his marriages sustained, now married to women of races forbidden under the Law given by

Moses. Were kings immune from the Law? The longer Solomon reigned, the more the presence and practices of foreign gods seemed to intrigue him, bringing his life very near to a point of renouncing Yahweh in favour of these diversions he had placed within the heart of his own personal life, and thus in the centre of his nation. God warned Solomon that the kingdom would be torn from his grasp and given to others if he carried on down this road. ☕ 6 Despite that warning, a promise was added that the covenant between God and David would hold firm, and a thread of succession was assured, come what may.

Nothing must be allowed to detract from Solomon's reign as a 'glory' period of history. Enterprises blossomed, both long-term and short-lived, his love of horses among them. Yet his achievements could not have gone ahead without the pre-existing trade routes and the goodwill of other nations and states, nor without the continuation of a period of peace from the power blocs of old, which would surely reappear again very shortly. How long would they stay dormant like sleeping volcanoes?

Because Solomon had opted not to develop the empire of his father by further war-making, the spoils of battle were no longer making contributions to the state treasury. ☕ 7 As the building of the temple proceeded the costs soared, as happens in so many modern construction projects. Is there nothing new in this world? The so-called free slave labour could not cover all the need. Solomon's own people were also pressed into service. No longer was the national income from road tolls on the foreign traders passing through the country enough to create a surplus. Corvée was the additional burden of the day – providing a day's unpaid work for the nation, or working in lieu of paying taxes that were due. The burdens of national policies and building projects were now impinging on, nay hurting, every inhabitant of the empire, and the seeds of uprising were well and truly sown in his core union lands of Israel and Judah. It could only be a matter of time before the powder keg of unrest blew. If ever the international situation reversed itself, and the core lands had demands of a foreign ruler imposed instead of being receivers of tribute, there would be nothing left from which it could be found. Would the 'defence only' policy of Solomon survive? Would the distracted and challenged faith of Solomon be enough for the nation under such conditions?

Attitudes Change

How, apart from taxation and work policies, had the rule of Solomon changed life for God's people? David had managed to unite very different religious approaches under the leadership of the monarch. Solomon allowed religious practices in his own household to challenge that unity. David could rely upon his closeness with the people to uphold religious unity. Solomon's more remote administrator's role allowed cracks of a serious nature to appear. He could be criticized for taking the Egyptian Pharaoh or the king of Tyre as role models of 'absolutism' in the kingly office, instead of allowing God to be the absolute ruler and guide of national affairs. A critical view of the building of the temple could claim it to be an example of his attitudes. The sanctuary and the royal palace were virtually the same united building. Was the sanctuary just a royal shrine? No, would come the reply, it was a place of worship for the people, but the critics had a point. Divinity and the office of king were in danger of merging, rather than assuring the humility of the person on the throne. ⌂ 8 It is interesting that the prophetic voices, heard in the times of David, seem to be almost silent during the early stories of Solomon, but awakened afresh as Solomon moved away from God. Had Solomon buried himself under the bureaucracy he had initiated and lost touch with the fundamental basics of kingship? Was the main emphasis of the nation now to be driven by mainly secular considerations? Oh that Samuel's powerful voice could again be heard as a means of guidance! Solomon had the ability to handle riddles and fables linked to abstract ideas, but his ability for contemplation on the God who is Creator and Ruler of all now seemed lacking.

| 9 | 2 | 2 | BC

The inevitable challenges to his rule had to come. Those 'thorns in the flesh' had not gone away. Nor had the matured young prince of Edom who had been living in Egypt. It would only take just one spark to set the over-taxed and over-burdened people into a flame of rebellion. Jeroboam was that spark, in the northern kingdom, Israel. Originally he had been a faithful worker who came to Solomon's attention as he worked on the walls of Jerusalem. He quickly rose to responsibility over the corvée system. He most certainly understood the resentment of the people to providing 'free' labour. Ahijah, a prophet from the religious centre of Shiloh, was also opposed to Solomon's approach. The two met on the road outside Jerusalem. The prophet tore his garment into twelve pieces, handing ten of them to Jeroboam as a sign that God would give that number of tribes to him as the new king. In fact, he was to go one tribe better than that. But here was God's warning on the verge of fulfilment. The important symbol for the future of God's people was thus in division. The united monarchy under David had almost come to a point of disintegration under the so-called glories of Solomon's reign. His personal actions and the seething discontent of the people were in danger of becoming focused upon religion. But would a freshly divided kingdom fare any better in leadership that could focus with clarity upon God? It would have to try, for 1 Kings 11 terminates the story of Solomon abruptly, simply saying that Solomon slept with his ancestors and his son Rehoboam succeeded him. What a task now lies ahead!

Chapter 6 Questionline

The questions that arise from this chapter mainly surround expectations of quality of life.

☕ 1a, 1b In protecting qualities and expectations of life, war has often been resorted to. The taking of human life in a battle situation is felt to be justified. What sort of guidelines are necessary to create such a

justification, and where could they come from in a multi-faith society?
Bible Notes ✎ ***2 Samuel 18:19–33***

☕ 2 Lifestyles change with each generation. Our expectations of quality and basic affluence are amended with them. How much can we afford to imitate our parents, or previous generations? Does their example always stand for right values?
Bible Notes ✎ ***1 Kings 3:1–9; 2 Chronicles 1:2–13***

☕ 3 What is the quality of peace that is so important? Then and now, what created a quiet life for one group of people shaped the lives of others into disruption and conflict. Can peace for all ever be achieved?
Bible Notes ✎ ***1 Kings 4:20–28***

☕ 4 The structure and quality of worship and religious life has, for centuries, depended upon a distinct role for priests, set apart and ordained to the office to which they have been called. The training given to the clergy no longer sets them aside as the educated elite in society. What does this mean? Are the laity now able to assume some or all of their roles? Would such an action improve the quality of our worship?
Bible Notes ✎ ***1 Kings 8:1–13; 2 Chronicles 5:2–6:2***

☕ 5 Unemployment, it seems, was unlikely to be a problem with all this work available. So different today, with world-wide shifts in skills radically changing patterns and qualities of life. The old Protestant work ethic implied that people were inferior if they did not earn their keep. What values would replace it today?
Bible Notes ✎ ***1 Kings 9:26–8***

☕ 6 Many tensions in the modern world have religious differences at their historical roots, or differences for which religion is blamed. Is it time for the different world religions to unite in some form of concord? How would Solomon's problems be avoided if we want to go on ensuring witness to 'the one true God'?
Bible Notes ✎ ***1 Kings 11:1–13***

7 The construction of items required to make war has always created riches for individuals and nations providing armaments. At the same time, those goods provide misery to the quality of life of innocent people caught up in conflict. Is there any way round such inequalities?
An ethical question

8 Humility is a quality of life. Does this always mean letting the will of others override our own contribution? Do we allow ourselves and our faith to appear trivial by stress on humility rather than having positive approaches to the challenges of modern life?
Bible Notes ✎ 1 Kings 10:23–5

Chapter 6 Bible Search

Solomon prays for wisdom as king	1 Kings 3:1–15; 2 Chronicles 1:2–13
Solomon's temple and palace	1 Kings 6:1–7:11; 2 Chronicles 3:1–14
Commercial development	1 Kings 9:26–8; 2 Chronicles 8:17–18
The errors and opponents of Solomon	1 Kings 11:1–40
The death of Solomon	1 Kings 11:43

Theme Prayer

Loving Father God, I offer to you all the gifts and abilities which reside in my life, my ability to think, my ability to affect the lives of others for good. Forgive me when I overlook that these and my many other abilities are from you and reside in me only as an act of your creative grace. Help me to use life fully and properly. Amen.

Chapter 7 Preview

In the next three hundred years or so, international structures changed, and the once mighty empire founded by David with them. Israel and Judah 'enjoyed' almost forty different rulers, who can be summarized with their approximate dates as an aid to walking through the maze. Where there are alternative names for the same person, they are shown in brackets. Dotted lines indicate the historical phases or time zones described on page 110.

BC	NORTHERN KINGDOM, ISRAEL	SOUTHERN KINGDOM, JUDAH
922	Jeroboam 1	Rehoboam
915		Abijam (Abijah)
913		Asa
901	Nadab	
900	Baasha	
877	Elah	
876	Zimri	
876	Omri, Tibni	
873		Jehoshaphat
869	Ahab	
850	Ahaziah	
849	Jehoram (Joram) brother of Ahaziah	Jehoram son of Jehoshaphat
842	Jehu	Ahaziah
842		Athaliah
837		Jehoash (Joash)
815	Jehoahaz	
801	Jehoash	
800		Amaziah
786	Jeroboam 2	
783		Uzziah (Azariah)
746	Zechariah	
745	Shallum	
745	Menahem	
742		Jotham
738	Pekahiah	
737	Pekah	
735		Ahaz
732	Hoshea	
721	*Fall of Samaria*	
715		Hezekiah
687		Manasseh
642		Amon
640		Josiah
609		Jehoahaz (Shallum)
609		Jehoiakim
598		Jehoiachin (Coniah)
597		Zedekiah
587		*Fall of Jerusalem*

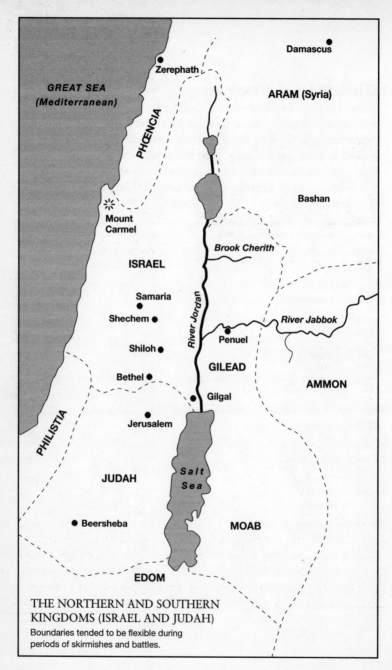

GREAT SEA
(Mediterranean)

Damascus

Zerephath

PHŒNICIA

ARAM (Syria)

Bashan

Mount
Carmel

Brook Cherith

ISRAEL

Samaria

Shechem

River Jabbok

Shiloh

Penuel

River Jordan

Bethel

GILEAD

Gilgal

AMMON

Jerusalem

PHILISTIA

*Salt
Sea*

JUDAH

Beersheba

MOAB

EDOM

THE NORTHERN AND SOUTHERN
KINGDOMS (ISRAEL AND JUDAH)

Boundaries tended to be flexible during
periods of skirmishes and battles.

Chapter 7

Law, Order and Worship

Bible Account

1 Kings
2 Kings
2 Chronicles
Amos (Israel)
Hosea (Israel)
Early Isaiah (Judah)
Micah (Judah)
Zephaniah (Judah)
Habakkuk (Judah)
Jeremiah (Judah)
Lamentations
Nahum

Author's Note

As illustrated above, the sources for the next phase of history are many, and it is inevitable – since these have been written at different stages – that conflicts in the order of events will occur. Academic discussion has not been ignored, but the storyline has been allowed to flow without such views being allowed to create intrusion.

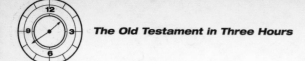
STORYLINE

O h what a complicated pattern now evolves. The story takes on a whole host of potential journey lines. It could be traced through the annals of Israel, the northern kingdom. Or through Judah, the southern kingdom. It could be traced through military endeavour. There are developments of the story through shifts in the international struggle for power. Or, finally, the historical journey could be revealed through emerging spiritual voices.

Whenever a single view of history is taken there is a certainty of distortion. All of these threads must be allowed to weave themselves into a single fabric of events. The preview to this chapter allows the story to unfold in time zones, rather than allow any one view to predominate. The first begins with the division of the kingdom after Solomon, through to the rules of the Jehorams. The second takes us forward to the fall of Samaria, and finally we follow the history of Judah to the fall of Jerusalem.

| 9 | 2 | 2 | BC

Phase One: North

Jeroboam has already emerged as a gifted leader with a heart of understanding towards the burdens placed upon community life, work and taxation. So greatly did he appreciate the people's difficulties that he covertly rebelled against Solomon, and was forced to flee to the protection of Egypt until King Solomon died. While waiting in the wings of history, he'd cemented his place with the Egyptian royal court by marrying Pharaoh's sister-in-law and had a child by her, who unfortunately later died.

There were skirmishes between Israel and Judah. Despite that, there were also hopes that the two could live together. King Rehoboam came to the throne and received representations on behalf of the hard-pressed northern people, and Jeroboam, having returned home, was associated with the effort. The unfavourable reception to the representations meant that the seething people moved to the verge of revolt. Jeroboam was summoned to a meeting of the northern tribes, and by acclaim was made their king.

The people's desire to leave behind what felt like stifling centralized bureaucracy based on Jerusalem was just part of a groundswell of separatist views in the north, which posed an immediate practical problem. Jerusalem was at the heart of both religious and political power, thanks to the combination of David's foresight and the administrative prowess of Solomon. The city could not equally serve two separate kingdoms. The southerners of Judah had been David's allies from the start. Their claim to Jerusalem as a capital city meant that a reinvigorated and fortified Shechem became the northern capital, with Penuel providing a second northern city of power covering administrative focus on the other side of the Jordan river.

Under Jeroboam's reign there was an element of religious reform in Israel. A question hangs over such work, surrounding the interpretation of faith in symbolic format. The bull had been a symbol of homage since at least the time of Moses. Even in those days, trade marks and logos had an importance. Judah used a winged lion symbol, linked to the Ark of the Covenant. Israel, under Jeroboam, adopted the bull – a sacrificial animal, but also one heavily significant in the worship of fertility gods of other religions. While such outward signs may appear insignificant, their importance lies in the fact that the worship of God was now divided in style. The north had no equivalent to the Ark of the Covenant for its new religious centres, Bethel and Dan. Their chosen symbol of the bull was reminiscent of a golden calf in the times of Aaron (Exodus 32). 📖 1 That bull had proved a distraction from the worship of God. The expressions of religious separation now looked as irreversible as the secular and civic division of the once united peoples.

Tensions lay ahead, for the elevation of Jeroboam to kingship broke the God-given line of Davidic succession for the north. There were to be many fierce physical battles between the two nations, but spiritual tensions have their birth at this point. Could a king

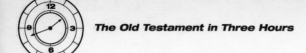

appointed by acclamation alone still preside in worship in the role of priest? And if he did so, would the altar at which he presided have implications in its future that would mean it had become defiled? A lot of clarification needed to be undertaken, but events were to preclude such action.

Over the kings who followed him it might perhaps be best to draw a veil – the way to the throne too often came through the murder of the current holder. As a result, the length of tenure on the throne could be very short, sometimes a matter of days. However, before turning to the significance of Ahab, a glance at the southern kingdom is helpful.

Phase One: South

Rehoboam, the son of Solomon, was crowned king, but despite being forty-one years of age when stepping into his father's shoes he was hesitant and lacking in positive thinking. Advisors abounded, but could not agree on their advice when attempting a unified message to their national leader. While Solomon's strong personality held the nation in check in former days, the changed nature of the new king allowed seething rebellion a chance to exert itself. What a blunder the new king made in telling the people he was going to add to their burdens – scorpions, he threatened, instead of whips. In that one small sentence he had created the division between north and south. Attempts to discipline the north led to him hiding himself in Jerusalem, muttering words about retaking the north, words that were never followed up by deeds. Had Jeroboam asked his family and friends in Egypt for back-up? There were clear warning noises coming at Rehoboam, who responded by making even stronger the defensive cities his father had provided. The constant battles between Israel and Judah over their joint borders now required a splitting of the new king's army to cover both northern threats and other rumblings from the south.

To make matters worse, the international power bloc situation began a significant shift. The low ebb of other powers had enabled David's empire to rise. But already Aram (Syria) was lost and fast becoming a power source in its own right, with Damascus as its core. The Philistines had obtained autonomy in the south, while the Ammonites and Moabites refused to accept Israel's rule over them. Rehoboam came under military onslaught from Egypt as part of a package of their re-emerging dreams of empire. Their bloody northward push engulfed the Philistines, swept through Judah and, surprisingly, also engulfed much of Israel. My, how Jeroboam must have felt sore about that! Family ties, it seems, count for little under war situations.

That destructive infiltration came to an end. The dreaded need for the payment of tribute by Jerusalem to Egypt now became a reality. Could the national budget stand it? A constructive infiltration was to follow on a spiritual level. Judah was on a low ebb of worship when Rehoboam came to the throne, because of Solomon's earlier interest in other religions. Jeroboam's changed status and religious emphasis in the north may have caused a migration of priests to the south. It is a matter of debate how helpful this was to religious strengths in the south. Over the years, the effects of changed religious attitudes in the north were to be significant, and these require a return to consider the north, to Israel, and to the times of King Ahab.

Phase One: North

To the north-west of Israel lay the lands of the Phoenician peoples. To the north-east, and mainly the opposite side of the Jordan, were the Arameans. Cross the Salt Sea from Judah and there lay the Moabites. And immediately across the Jordan were the Ammonites. The people of Aram were to be hostile throughout Ahab's reign.

Omri had been a highly respected king, within Israel and abroad. His hold upon kingship, however, contained an element of discomfort, for a rival by the name of Tibni was equally sought as ruler by the people, and both men appear to have reigned over the same nation at the same time, resulting in a civil war situation. Omri was technically a foreigner who had shown prowess in battle and was promoted to be king during one such foray. Among his significant acts was the movement of the capital to Samaria, a name that became used on an interchangeable basis with 'Israel'. One

part of the biblical record makes Omri evil in the sight of God. It is important to recognize the fact that he managed friendly relationships with Judah, turned Moab into a subject people, and began to do the same towards Aram. This was part of a period of new conquests and strengthening of the kingdom. His alliance with Phoenicia included the marriage of his son Ahab with Jezebel, the daughter of the king of Tyre. How many more of these alliances would happen before the pitfalls were understood? Putting these two together may have been good for strengthening the reign of Omri, but became a ticking time bomb of disaster for the nation's future.

869 BC

To be called a Jezebel implies a shameless, immoral stance to life. Here is the source of the term of disgrace. Looking back at history with the gift of hindsight can bring frustration, for the mistakes are all too obvious. One thing was to Jezebel's credit: she was devout in religious worship. The frustrating problem it created was the repeat of an old one – she quite naturally worshipped the gods she had grown up with, those of Tyre, Baal-Melcarth and Asherah among them. In all probability the latter was a mother god and thus associated strongly with fertility. Such worship contained many acts that gave Jezebel the immoral reputation she retains. Asherah, partner of El, is credited in ancient documents with being the mother of seventy gods, including Baal. El is a fairly normal Middle Eastern name for a god, and it was often applied to Yahweh. How was the ordinary man in the street to sort out the implications of the name without a degree in theology?

The very things that had brought Solomon's rule into question are now put back at the centre of northern military-style leadership. The problem with Jezebel was that this was not a personal religion for her: she was an evangelist with fervour and enthusiasm. Like many a dutiful husband, Ahab wanted to please his wife and built a place of Baal worship in the heart of Samaria. If he'd meant it to stop there he was wrong, for it spawned a huge supporting college of prophets of Baal. He became a personal convert within his wife's evangelical outreach. The potential for the loss of worship of Yahweh, the one true God of Israel's fathers, was a very real peril. Yet to worship the same gods as those who might attack you brought a measure of hoped-for security and unity. Surely Baal could not be on two sides at the same time?

Those who expected faith in God to wane were in for a big surprise. The long years of quiet levels of activity from prophets among God's people were about to come to an abrupt end. If Jezebel was an enthusiast for her religion, there emerged a person of yet greater zeal towards Yahweh. His name was Elijah. For most of his life he seems to have been a solitary and strange person, with gifts and abilities to work miracles. In common with prophetic practice, his actions could at times include ecstatic dancing similar to that of the Muslim whirling dervishes. Prophets were known to make weird noises within their activities, to cut themselves, and in general to be men of mystery. Elijah would have been viewed no differently. ⌨ 2

Having warned King Ahab that a big drought was about to decimate the country, Elijah took refuge in places God had prepared for him, for droughts were far from uncommon. His salvation was initially through bird food, at the Brook Cherith (Wadi Yabis), but as the drought bit harder he was guided towards a hard-pressed widow and her son at Zarephath – as the crow flies, a distance of around one hundred and fifteen kilometres, or seventy miles. Through his presence their meagre rations renewed themselves by daily miracle with a sufficiency that covered Elijah's needs as well. Tragedy struck when the child died, and with the application of what some view as a precursor of modern emergency resuscitation procedures, Elijah restored breathing to the youngster. On a number of occasions the miracles included the presence of fire, so often – with thunder, raging storms, volcanic eruptions or lightning flashes – portrayals in the Old Testament of the actual presence of God in a specific unfolding event. These events have often been associated with sources linked to the covenant relationship between God and his people. Elijah had come to realize that the old Mosaic covenant with God was threatened by the recognition of Baal beyond just local shrines into what had become the new state religion.

A change to the power pictures of a God imposing himself upon a frightened human race came to Elijah. The old sense of power in fire had just been seen as Elijah clashed with the school of Baal priests on or by Mount Carmel. The priests of Baal prepared a sacrifice, but failed to call down fire from heaven to consume it. Elijah had his sacrifice ready, drenched in water for good measure. And God's symbolic presence was revealed in its fiery consummation. The destruction of the credibility and life of the Baal priests may have been partly lost as the pernicious power of the drought ended, but the rage of Jezebel burned with venom. Elijah had flown the flag of challenge to the people to choose afresh the God of their forefathers. Jezebel's threats upon Elijah's life drove him into a period of retreat, first to Beersheba in Judah, but then on the long trek further south into the Sinai desert, and to Mount Horeb. He took refuge in a cave, but the powers of wind, earthquake and fire did not this time contain the comfort of God's close proximity. In the silence that followed, the presence of God came in dialogue, and Elijah let his inner feelings of being the last person faithful to God flow out. In the sound of sheer silence that followed such a statement, God made it known to him that he was far from alone, for seven thousand was the size of the righteous remnant Elijah had overlooked. ⬛ 3

Are we to read anything into the fact that the first act of Elijah on coming out of his self-enforced isolation was to break his near solitary work-style, and call Elisha as a partner and eventual successor? The tensions between Ahab and Jezebel on one hand, and Elijah with Elisha on the other, were to remain through times of battle and in clashes over Ahab's unethical behaviour towards Naboth, a man who wanted to maintain the purity of ancestral property rights against the wishes and desires of the king. Ahab eventually died in disgrace before God, and in another upsurge of battles with the armies of Aram. His son Ahaziah came to the throne, and repeated Baal worship and other failures of his father.

Israel may not have been finding strength in kingship at this stage, but she had raised up within herself a spiritual champion in Elijah to oppose the prophets of Baal. But would anyone care any more? Was religion, which had fallen into the doldrums of public awareness, to stay there for ever? Elijah's surprising release from his work by being taken up into heaven left a new champion of God's presence among the people – Elisha, also a man of miracles. Curing leprosy, restoring life to a child, feeding a large number of men with little more than twenty loaves of barley, the stories attributed to him reveal an important facet of religious development. Elisha was clearly bonded into some form of a prophetic school or guild. His humanity there and in the wider community made him a source of inspiration to people growing in the true faith, despite all the influences of foreign gods. He proclaimed the will of God with a force powerful enough to carve into the character of the nation a mark of hope for the future. They would need it.

Phase One: The Pressures on Both Nations

The international threat had been brewing in an ominous way for some time, but from a new direction. Egypt's threats were temporarily on the wane. In the time of Ahab, the Arameans had become an enemy. Invasions into Israel brought defeat to the king of Damascus. The power of Assyria was always in the background, and alliances between Israel and Judah to maintain relationships were always under tension. But the same could be said of treaties with other states and nations that could be torn up and remade elsewhere when mood suited the needs of one nation. This was a dangerous age, in which everyone had to watch their backs.

The threads of history change and concentrate on spiritual developments, the foundations for which Elijah and Elisha have prepared.

Phase Two: North

```
8 4 2
```
BC

The weary trail of assorted kings continued. Their expertise and longevity on the throne varied. Jehu had been put on the throne by Elijah (an alternative account involves Elisha, by proxy) – perhaps there was a glimmer of hope here of a man who would stay close to Yahweh. There was a desperate need of reform in the nation. Instead of fulfilling potential, his response emerged in the form of murder towards everyone who didn't agree with him. More dashed hopes.

There were voices issuing warnings to the nation. Not about external threats, but things which were of far more vital internal importance. The first was that of Amos. Hosea was not far behind. Jeroboam 2 had been king for a number of years. He'd recovered lands lost to other nations. The boundaries of his nation were expanding slowly. Egyptian power was in decline. Surprisingly, the Assyrian revival was weakening its grip. They were too busy dealing with problems elsewhere in their territory. Some glimpses of resurgent hope came to the surface. The arts flourished. International trade showed signs of recovery. Israel could again take charge of the trade routes that passed through her borders. The secular sides of the nation had signs of life in them, and the prosperity of people bounded back to a liberality at least equal to that which some of them had enjoyed during Solomon's time. Hope for worship surrounded the great temple at Bethel, which was now hard pressed to cope with the demands of worship. The payment of tithes, observance of festivals and pilgrimages were fulfilled. With all this going right for a change, what did these two prophets, Amos and Hosea, think they were doing? Were they just a couple of spoil-sports or kill-joys? No: there was in the affluence of the age a tense mixture of religion and emergent nationalism. ⬛ 4 Under such circumstances it was still much too easy for secular matters to take priority over faith in Yahweh.

Amos may not have regarded himself as a prophet, but history has bestowed upon him the high respect of that office. His denial may have had a lot to do with the fact that the upswing of religious worship of the age was totally misguided. It was addressed to Yahweh, but in fact was almost totally reflecting the practice of Canaanite worship and Baal, confirmed by the pictures of the time presented by Hosea. This change led to a very different and detrimental view of society to that developed within Mosaic faith. Even the guilds of prophets which had been present for long years in Israel's history had allowed themselves to be absorbed into outwardly attractive new religious practices. Amos challenged inner commitment, and had to separate himself from some fellow prophets as a result. For him the practice of wild music to induce trances was not a focus on Yahweh. To Amos fell the burden of restarting the prophetic voice. The more he looked at religious observance and community life, the more he changed his words from ones of hope into pictures of gloom and doom – yet a doom that remained under God's control. Perhaps his perspective on life and religion could be distinct from the old prophets because he was never trained to be one. He was a shepherd, and thus a natural observer of life. His heart rested in the ways of God, and his longing was for a return to a united people as in the times of David, and the purity of worship of that era.

Amos gave to the people of his time, and to the later Christian Church, a development in the understanding of the nature of God. Because Israel had had a special relationship with God, her responsibilities in fulfilling the will of God were increased. Amos saw that God controlled the lives of all nations, so he could raise up any one of them in acts of judgement upon those who failed to achieve the standards expected of them. Concepts of the doctrine of election, outside the scope of a book that seeks to remain 'basic', lie within the teachings of Amos and deserve careful consideration by people of faith searching for a right relationship with God.

The physical earthquake that shook the nation just two years into Amos's work was nothing to the shaking that was to fall upon his personal life as a result of his pronouncements of doom. Critics are never popular if their words are not desired by the majority. To talk of an invader coming to ruin life seemed designed to create a backlash. To predict the fall of the king was to invite an accusation of treason. This prophet could not be bought. He would not change his pronouncements to happy words of national commendation. Some of the other prophets undoubtedly would have done, both to line their pockets and to create an easier style of life. Banishment from the nation into Judah would not silence the man. What was it that stirred him so much?

He saw dishonesty among the judges of the time. Tip them a few extra Euros, pounds or dollars and you were assured of a ruling in your favour. Provided, of course, that the other party had not upped the stakes beyond yours! He saw businessmen achieving results by the most doubtful of means. Riches were coming into their pockets by any methods they could devise. Worse – those riches were going into very few pockets, draining resources from the poor and needy in the land. The split between the 'haves' and the 'have-nots' was widening by the day. Small farmers found their land stripped from them by the rich barons of the age, changing the farmers into little better than serfs. The once-honest nation was totally and utterly bent. And the inner burden of Amos verbally burst out upon festivals and religious gatherings, challenging the rich, the priests and the misguided prophets. He issued more than just a challenge, going as far as accusing the nation of failing to meet the basic principles of humanity, biting words to a people who felt called to be the special nation under God. The prophet's words were not restricted to his own people, but were addressed to other surrounding nations. Frustratingly for the prophet, within his own nation was a comfortable feeling that they were 'religious', and therefore had to be right. Amos could view this contemptuous approach to God with nothing other than a fear for the end of his world. Catastrophe. Unless, that is, the nation would accept judgement upon itself.

Just twenty years after one gloom merchant, another – Hosea – added to their discomfort. The luxury of Jeroboam's rule had gone, and international threats were looming. One king after another had tried to rule the nation, six in all, and attempts were being made to stave off impending disaster by seeking dubious alliances with other nations wherever and whenever they could, one minute trying to buy off Assyria and another appealing to Egypt. Hosea, like Amos before him, tried to focus the attention of the people on God and away from the salvation potential of other nations. But the political leaders of the time continued to switch and change their views and alliances, grasping at proverbial straws in the wind. To all effects the nation was crashing downhill leaderless. Hosea could see the inner effect of injustice among the people, but he expressed it in kinder, more considerate terms than the blunt Amos. He illustrated his presentation by personal pictures of unfaithfulness through broken marriage. God was likened to a husband to the people, wed to them in the early days of Moses. Now the honeymoon was over, and the people were rejecting or ignoring the marriage covenant. Amos had seen only doom. Hosea could see it, but beyond the doom came his vision of a new dawn. He called for faith, on the basis that a return to God is a return to the source of love.

The voices, iron Amos and pleading Hosea, were to no avail. The international tensions eventually spilled over into the northern nation. Assyria had regained its strength. There was a lethargy within Israel that the injustices under which they lived could be made no worse by the potential invasion of troops. It came, and a systematic deportation of useful citizens began. The prophetic threat of exile had become reality. The old nation of Israel, weakened by injustice and internal revolutions, now became absorbed into the life of more powerful ones, leaving Judah to the south as the only remnant people of Yahweh. The lands of Israel were to become settlement areas for displaced people from Aram and later for Arabs, and there is some evidence that defeated Babylonians were also exiled into the lands of Israel. It is a cruel irony that as the exiled people of Israel eventually disappeared into obscurity in Media, their own land was being repopulated with exiles from other lands, and by peoples who were destined now to live alongside the remnant Israelite population as a mixed and alien people. ☕ 5

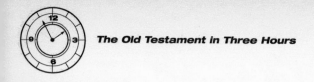

Phase Three: South

 BC

Despite the problems in the north, relationships between the two parts of God's people had improved. The affluence one nation enjoyed, the other also shared. But with the eventual fall of Israel, Judah became the new, and even smaller, buffer between Egypt in the south and the Assyrian power that had taken Israel. Those two power blocs had no love for each other. However, the Assyrians had deep problems as their empire boundaries expanded. Babylon was another nation they had absorbed, and it was restless under the yoke. Unlike Israel, it had retained some degree of inner strength.

Hezekiah ruled on the throne of Judah. He attempted religious reform, the success of which was very varied around the nation. The prophetic voice was certainly present in Judah. Micah drew on the northern experience in his efforts to turn religion back to responsiveness before Yahweh.

Hezekiah's aim was to upgrade political and military abilities in the nation. The creation of a watercourse into Jerusalem may have looked a strange thing to do at such a time, and some may have muttered the words 'waste of money'. But what a bonus it would become later on. His reign was a busy one. Egypt and Ethiopia's combined strength were always tempting as allies. So was the restless Babylonian spirit. Rebellion against Assyria would, if they could create the right combination between these groupings, be a practical possibility. Was the time right, and could the king rely on such people? Having seen Israel fall, these allies would have to be one hundred per cent reliable if the stranglehold of Assyria was to be broken.

The prophetic voice enters these national events with tones of opposition – to ideas of rebellion. Were prophets also politicians? What right did they have to deal with military matters? The prophet involved was Isaiah. ☕ 6 Some forms of scholarship would respond, 'Which Isaiah?', claiming there were three, and dividing up the book named after him into specified chapters, some allocated to this period, some to the times of exile that were to come, and other passages to the years after the exile. While we must respect the force of such an academic exercise, within each section the dating of chapters is hotly disputed. A prophetic school of thought, over the next period of history, may have taken Isaiah's name to itself. This is a common and respectable procedure, not intended to deceive. Most prophets had disciples. So, in weaving a path through this section of history and maintaining a basic storytelling stance, it is more to the point to refer simply to 'early' Isaiah.

Early Isaiah was most certainly opposed to rebellion against Assyria. In the end, events took over, for Assyria marched into Palestine while Egyptian and Ethiopian troops moved threateningly northwards – this time to defeat. Judah was but a pawn in a game over which troops could argue. They could do very little to help themselves. The scene was set for some very tense sets of negotiations, in which Isaiah was to play a significant part.

From the start he spoke out, as had the prophets in the north, bringing charges of social injustice and religious apathy. He is a complex character who seems to have had close access both to religious and court life and to the king. So he was no ordinary man in the street, but perhaps a priest and a member of the nobility, for only such a combination might explain his unique position. He came to his special calling from God prior to the rule of Hezekiah and prior to the fall of the northern kingdom, but was in self-imposed withdrawal from public life, awaiting God's voice. He strongly urged Hezekiah to stay away from alliances with Egypt and Ethiopia, who were known to take any opportunity available to attack Assyria. Isaiah sensed that Assyria would be God's chosen means of rebuke to Judah, and that the nation's internal injustices needed God's stern discipline from this source.

As with both Amos and Hosea, Isaiah must not be seen just as a figure in a historical narrative. He had a profound effect on the development of an understanding of God within a rising tide of prophetic activity. His particular contribution was to focus attention on the person of God – his holiness and sovereign power

– and to make direct contrasts with human failure. Faith was his call to the people.

If the jest regarding the opening scenes of the Bible had the tabloids rushing to fill their columns with tales of nudity, they should be on the alert once again. Isaiah became deeply concerned with the dark omens both of the international tensions and of his own nation's state of depravity. For a three-year period he proclaimed his message stark naked. It got him noticed, but what his fellow members of the nobility would make of him one can only hazard a guess!

7 0 3 BC

Sargon, King of Assyria, a powerful military man who had many building projects to his credit – and one unused city to his discredit – met his death in a very minor military scrap. How unreasonable an end for a warrior of his status. But to those who hated Assyria here was the moment for which they had longed. King Hezekiah felt himself dragged into the resultant coalition to take advantage of a power vacuum. Isaiah could not remain silent, and likened the alliance to being thrown into hell. 'Egypt cannot be depended upon!' he exclaimed. The Assyrian military threat slowly strangled Judah. Hezekiah tried to buy his way out of trouble, promising to pay whatever tribute was demanded. To do so meant emptying the treasury, raiding the royal reserves and stripping the temple of all its valuables. The wealth of Judah was no more. As more events then unfolded, Hezekiah became trapped in Jerusalem by the encircling Assyrian armies that had moved down from the north. Thank goodness for that water supply he'd built! But what a turnabout, for it was to the prayers of Isaiah before God that the king turned. The Assyrian armies were hit by plague, and also had to shift quickly to confront a section of the Egyptian army, advancing on them from the south. ☕ 7 Jerusalem was saved, but what now lay before the nation?

Elsewhere, the Assyrians sustained a defeat at the hands of the rising Babylonian threat. Yet they were still strong enough to mount a second attack on Judah, and as Hezekiah's life ended, dark, menacing threats hung over the future. ⏛ 8

686 BC

Manasseh came to the throne at this difficult time, at only twelve years old. It is hardly surprising that he was influenced in favour of the pro-Assyrian section at court. They were strong, and to argue with such a nation seemed stupidity. Hezekiah's reforms to centralize the worship of Yahweh, and thus protect it, were turned on their head. Local shrines were again permitted, resulting in an inevitable, and uncontrolled, slide towards Baal worship. The Assyrian supremacy meant that their gods were worshipped, and, along with this, communication ceremonies to contact the dead, human sacrifice and prostitution were again seen in the nation.

As Manasseh grew, so did his reputation for brutality. To be a prophet in those days was to risk your very life. There remained a solid body of people loyal to Yahweh, so when the king was carried off into captivity, many felt it a just punishment. He somehow returned, repentant (according to the Chronicles account, but not confirmed in Kings), and in fairness did try to restore the worship of Yahweh.

These were difficult times, but some issues held a positive aspect for the nation. While they remained under the thumb of Assyria, Egypt weakened and fell to the same source of power. At least it was a bonus to have domination from just one source. But then ...

652 BC

...that seething, dominated powder keg of Babylon could contain itself no longer. Civil war broke out. From Assyria's point of view things went from bad to worse. Uprisings began among tribes in the Syrian desert, with more, similar events testing their patience in other places.

Manasseh may have joined in, for there was a restoration of his control over many fortified cities in Judah, and a strengthening of

125

defences, including those of Jerusalem. Egypt also managed to throw off the Assyrian shackles.

How far are we to respect the 'conversion' or restoration of Manasseh to the ways of Yahweh? If it was real, it seems to have had little effect on his family, for when son Amon came to the throne for two short years it was to the worship of Assyrian gods that he turned. A court intrigue probably brought about his murder. His eight-year-old son Josiah replaced him by popular demand. Perhaps his youth enabled him to make his own decisions about worship, for by the age of sixteen he was rejecting the Assyrian gods in favour of Yahweh. In the coming years he slowly gained control of lost territories of the old empire of David. Assyria by now was no longer the force she once was, weakened by uprisings and rebellions. Then came the best opportunity of spiritual revival in Judah for many a long year.

Out went Assyrian gods. Out went Canaanite worship ideas. Under Josiah's reign the old Book of the Law had been rediscovered. Was this what we might recognize as Deuteronomy, written in secret during the reign of Manasseh? The young king could now lead a total purge, so that restoration of proper worship of God could again become the focal point of national life. The same reformation movement spread into the former northern kingdom of Israel, alongside Josiah's ability to take back political power.

Mosaic religion was back, and the influence of the former work of the prophet Hosea was at the heart of it and in the heart of a man from Anathoth, near Jerusalem. His name was Jeremiah. He was a man with a deep sense of call from God, carrying with him the ability to speak in true prophetic style. His voice had been heard condemning social injustices for some while. But the reforms must have lifted his spirits. The records of Jeremiah's opinions around the time of the reformation are muted in the biblical record. We are to see much more of him after the time of Josiah's reign.

Meanwhile the international power struggle continued. The Medes started to exert an influence that over the next seventy-five years was to extend in a wide band from south of the Black Sea, expanding south of the Caspian Sea as far as the Persian Gulf, and eastwards into India, almost to the Indus river. It created a massive new empire to contend with, finally eclipsing the Assyrians. At home, Josiah was busy collecting all the old traditions to restore the stature and identity of his people.

It was around this period that the prophet Nahum wrote a vivid poem enthusiastically celebrating the downfall of the Assyrian Empire. Graphic portrayals of cavalry charges are intermixed with scenes of panic among the enemy. And the whole scene is attributed to God's actions, as the avenger on the nation's old immoral cruel enemy. What Nahum does not deal with are the faults in his own people, so was he unfair? As seen against modern ideas, perhaps he was. Not against his own time, for then to lay a curse on an enemy who had been so evil was a way of expressing total loyalty and appreciation of God.

6 0 9 BC

Assyrians, Babylonians, Medes, Egyptians and a host of other international movements created a series of events as struggles towards a new pattern of Middle Eastern control unravelled. Josiah had to be constantly alert in protecting the independence he had gained both for his own people and for the extended influence over parts of David's old empire. The attempt came to disaster at Megiddo, when he tried to prevent the Egyptians and Assyrians linking together. He was killed, dying either on the battlefield or later, having been taken back in Jerusalem. There was huge and genuine mourning for him.

Jehoiakim eventually came to the throne, but right from the moment of his coronation the figure of Jeremiah emerged from the shadows to begin to deal with some wrong religious notions. What had developed since their reformation was an almost magical belief that the ceremonies themselves were the core of worship. What this sensitive and passionate man had to do was to prepare the people to understand the love of God and the person of God, for he sensed that in front of them was the most testing disaster so far in the

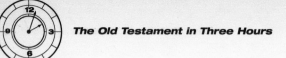

whole history of God's people. They would need to feel the actual personal presence of Yahweh if they were to cope.

His role was to take him into great personal danger. At one time he was thrown into a stinking squelching pit, and on another put in the stocks and left overnight. His sensitive nature was badly affected; times of apparent depression flowed over him, and he lamented life itself. Here was a man who felt the presence of Yahweh so close that a constant flow of dialogue was possible. Here also was a man to whom doubt and faith were alternating companions. Here was a man who knew from personal experience the closeness of God, which he longed to communicate.

What must have felt like the proverbial last straw to this man of intense religious fervour was the behaviour of the new king: party-loving, merrymaking, and with bestial brutality. The people continued down the mistaken road of worshipping the temple rather than God himself. The vital reformation was now fast slipping through the grasp of the nation, and no one seemed to realize the shallowness that was absorbing and shattering their religious life. They had lost the close connection between an ethical and moral lifestyle and the faith they expressed.

The constant pressure for reform that flowed from Jeremiah caused his expulsion from the temple. Under the guidance of God he withdrew and began the task of writing his messages down, charging his trusty companion Baruch to go in his place and read them to the people. They were both banished – hardly surprising given the conditions of the time. As the king listened to the content of Jeremiah's writings he took the opportunity to chop it into pieces, tossing each defiantly into the fire. Undaunted, Jeremiah and Baruch rewrote their important message.

Meanwhile, international tensions were building, following a massive clash at Carchemish. The Egyptian army is reputed to have been totally slaughtered. Seeing fresh dangers, Jeremiah bravely stormed back to public life and proclaimed that doom was about to befall the nation. Still the people vilified him. Still they poured scorn on him. His response was to enter a time of grief and of confession before God. His aching heart came to near breaking point, turning on God with accusations of deception. Moods change, and he also had moments of compassionate appreciation towards the life around him, and God at the heart of it.

5 9 8 BC

In the light of the massive tensions outside the nation, one can hardly credit that this was the moment Jehoiakim chose to refuse tribute demanded by Babylon. Could he really have been surprised that these bully-boys brought a terrible siege upon Jerusalem? Jeremiah uttered more words about the nation's loss of closeness with God, but it was too late now. King Jehoiachin, son of Jehoiakim, was taken captive to Babylon, and there was no time for anyone to fill his shoes properly before deportation began. Would we now give this event the name 'ethnic cleansing'? A host of prophets came to the forefront, talking of their return in the immediate future. Jeremiah knew better, and made dramatic efforts to influence a gathering of smaller nations eager to combine their strength and defeat Babylon. He wrote letters to the exiles telling them not to believe false prophets.

The homeland situation grew ever darker. Jeremiah was arrested for desertion – or so the charge against him read. And from prison he began pleading for the nation to surrender to Babylon. Interviews with the new king, Zedekiah, who was by now in depression himself, brought no instant solution. There was none. The invading troops poured into the city, and for all normal purposes Judah had joined its partner peoples of Israel in obscurity. More exiles occurred. How much worse could life possibly get? Not much, might be Jeremiah's view in Lamentations (assuming him to be the author, that is). God seemed to have deserted the people, whose agony cried out in humiliation.

Is there no hope in Israel? Are God's promises to Abraham and Moses now totally undermined? ⌨ 9

Chapter 7 Questionline

In this chapter there has been an interweaving of two themes in the struggling life of two nations. The first combines civic, ethical and moral behaviour patterns. The second is that of worship and witness. As the quality and sincerity of worship improved, the national status and affluence also seemed to be rising. But it worked in the downward direction as well. The questions that follow focus attention on these areas of modern life.

1 The importance of having a visible sign of the presence of God must not be dismissed as unimportant to spiritual development. Many parts of the Church have grown up expressing themselves in visual ways, through statues, candles and icons, for example. The symbolism of the cross is vital to a majority of Christians. Yet other churches reject these, along with gowns and clerical collars, even the courtesy title of 'Reverend' for the minister. By rejecting, have we put our nation in danger of missing out on the visible presence of spirituality?
Bible Notes ✎ *1 Kings 12:25–33*

2 Some acts within worship have enlivened the atmosphere from the stolid pattern of earlier generations. It is not unusual to incorporate dancing, clapping and crying out 'Amen'. Others incorporate the making of unintelligible noises and the frenzied throwing of people on the floor. Some practise the speaking and interpreting of tongues, others seek healing by laying hands on the needy.

How would a new enquirer after faith find these practices, or our talk of 'the body and blood of Christ' in Holy Communion? How do we define what is acceptable and proper practice in worship?
Bible Notes ✎ *1 Kings 17:1–7; 18:30–39*

3 The place of silence and retreats as part of the broad spectrum of worship does not always have a high profile in

importance. Are we afraid of silence in the modern world? Does silence enable God's voice to be heard? Are we afraid of what we might hear?

Bible Notes ✎ ***1 Kings 19:1–16***

🖺 4 The mixture of zeal in religious belief often goes hand in hand with national pride in the modern world. Nations, or sections of or within nations, too easily separate themselves from others on ethnic, religious or nationalistic ideals. What can we do to avoid faith becoming a source of division? What can we do to avoid our chosen worship styles becoming sources of division within the unity of the Church?

Bible Notes ✎ ***Amos 5:1–7; Hosea 6:1–6***

🖺 5 We often think of living in a multi-faith society as a problem of the modern world. This whole chapter refutes that concept. What can we learn from our Old Testament characters about dangers – and opportunities? Can a person belonging to a faith that ignores Jesus Christ truly be our 'neighbour' in the New Testament sense? Is it right to promote one religion as superior to, or more effective than, another?

Bible Notes ✎ ***Hosea 9:1–6; 10:1–3***

🖺 6 The role of the prophet is fundamental to this phase of Old Testament history. Many characters from Moses onwards were regarded as prophets. How do we define the role and responsibility of a prophet? Prophecy has been regarded as one of the gifts of the Holy Spirit in the Christian Church since its birth. How is prophecy achieved today? Is it really appropriate to make pronouncements in the name of God on matters of military strategy or political issues? The Church is sometimes accused of silence in these matters – does that mean we have lost the gift of prophecy, and the relevance of the Bible to modern life?

Bible Notes ✎ ***Isaiah 6:1–8; compare Ezekiel 1:4–28]***

7 Prayer is an important part of both public worship, and personal devotions. How do we define an answer to prayer? How do we decide what we should pray for? In this part of the story we can see the hand of God providing relief to his hard-pressed people. But do we also attribute the terrible results of plague to his hand?

Bible Notes ✎ **2 Kings 19:35**

8 There is a theme running through much of this part of history that other nations are being used to discipline Israel and Judah because of their low moral, ethical and spiritual levels. Can such an analysis of events be sustained? What sort of God is portrayed by such actions – are we back to the punishing God of Genesis? How does God bring discipline to people of faith in the modern world?

Bible Notes ✎ **2 Kings 20:1-7; 2 Chronicles 32:24-6; Isaiah 38:1-8**

9 Can our failures of faith affect, or undermine, the purposes of God to humankind?

Chapter 7 Bible Search

Northern tribes break from Judah	1 Kings 12; 2 Chronicles 10
Ahab's marriage to Jezebel	1 Kings 16:31–4
Elijah and the drought	1 Kings chapter 17
Elijah confronts the priests of Baal	1 Kings 18:20–46
Elijah flees from Jezebel	1 Kings 19:1–18
Elisha, man of miracles	2 Kings chapter 4
Amos and the guilt of the people	Amos chapter 3
Restoration of Manasseh after repentance	2 Chronicles 33:10–20

Theme Prayer

Merciful Father, there is much about my worship of you that challenges my discipline. I do not always listen for your voice. I am sometimes too busy praying to listen. I cannot be silent. I am so sure my own pattern of worship is right that I do not consider what other styles have to say to my practices. Help me to worship you aright. Amen.

Chapter 8

New Millennium, New Milestones

Bible Account

Jeremiah
Ezekiel
Isaiah (of Consolation)
Haggai
Zechariah
Ezra chapters 1–6
Isaiah chapters 55–66
Malachi
Obadiah

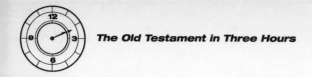

STORYLINE

They all have it. North Africa, the Seychelles, Spain, the West Indies. Sunshine, that is, and normally plenty of it. An essential ingredient for any holiday, and something upon which most people like to be able to rely. A chance to get away, to relax, to enjoy a different culture with a contrasting set of traditions. It's doubtful if many people actually philosophize about it, but the opportunity is also there to muse over one's own homeland in a way which can't be done while in the centre of familiar surroundings.

The exiles from Judah were not on holiday, but their hearts longed for Jerusalem, longed to see the twinkling of sunshine across the Salt Sea, longed for the best country ever – home. They yearned for the homeland that had been promised to them almost exactly one millennium before. At that time the separate tribes had been driven by the extremity of starvation into Egypt for survival. They had emerged from that experience of hard service as a people. Now again they were in a foreign land. Babylon. Again they were pressed into the service of another nation. Could history repeat itself? Could a new version of Moses lead them out of their new slavery into the Promised Land once more?

☐ 5 8 7 BC

Jerusalem, and the whole of Judah with it, had fallen into the hands of Babylon. The leaders of Judah had been taken into exile, and what remained at home was a leaderless people facing an uncertain future. Thousands had died in battle, and because of the disease and starvation which followed the disruption. Many had fled to the hills and desert to escape deportation, hoping to drift back when more peaceful times returned. Others sheltered in the lands of Ammon, Edom, Moab, Samaria, Galilee and the Transjordan. Edom seems a strange place to shelter, for Obadiah had been a strong critic of the Edomites. They had not come to the aid of Judah. Their continued hostility was inexcusable, for these were descendants of Esau

(Genesis 25:23) and should not, after all these centuries, have kept the old historical divisions between them going, most certainly not under current international tensions.

Reflections During Exile

Meanwhile, in Babylon the exiles went through a long reflective period concerning their homeland, their faith, their God; and for a great majority came the realization that it was their own actions that had put them in this position. 📖 1 A most uncomfortable admission. Yet dwelling in their hearts were the words they recalled had come to them in past days from Jeremiah, reminding them that God had promised that houses and fields and vineyards would again be bought and tended by them in their own land. Could they build their hopes on such promises? There were those other prophets still promising an immediate return. A far more attractive idea! But would a 'quick fix' really cure the fundamental problems they had experienced at home?

Nebuchadnezzar, the King of Babylonia, died in 562 BC and a series of pathetic rulers followed. Conditions of life in the whole area changed considerably for both local people and exiles. The loss of strong core directive rule often meant disorganized local communities and persecution of Jews for a short period of time. 📖 2 Daniel chapters 1 to 6 paints a picture of this period, although written at a different time (see Chapter 10).

Jeremiah had continued his links with the exiles for a while. He'd been allowed a measure of respect by the invaders when Jerusalem fell, having shown what was interpreted as sympathy to their aims. The potential existed for him to send them letters and messages as troops came and went. One such communication is included in Jeremiah chapter 29. Some of Judah's leaders were placed in exile prior to the fall of Jerusalem, and it was to these early departures that Jeremiah could pen words of hope. That was the first of three phases of exile, rather than there being one massive departure. The first was ten years before the fall of Jerusalem, the second at the fall, and the third about 582 BC.

Why, even allowing for their short period of persecution, were the

exiles so prone to feelings of depression and despair? 🖵 3 Their position of enforced residence in a foreign place must be high on the list of reasons. As the years rolled on, the false prophets' failed promises of an immediate return added to their sense of depression. The news filtering through that their once-proud city of Jerusalem now lay in ruins was a heavy and growing burden. As they reflected on their homeland and the life that might have been, they realized that long-held feelings of their nation as inviolable no longer held credibility. They remembered Yahweh's promise that the line of David would be upheld. Even that treasured idea was in ruins. The justice of God was easy to question in their low state of depression. Was even Yahweh helpless before Babylon? The warnings of Jeremiah now came back to haunt them. The words of Amos and Micah about responsibility to covenant law echoed through their minds.

Theological Reflections

But Jeremiah's work was not done. The messages to the exiles could not leave people without hope, nor for that matter must the same fate fall upon the people left in the homeland. His personal call to the service of God contained instructions both to 'uproot' and to 'tear down' on the one hand, but also to 'build' and to 'plant'. It was to the second part of his ministry of restoration that life now pointed. 🖵 4 Remaining in the homeland, he could use correspondence and personal witness to lift the people's perceptions of life and spirituality. The need was the same at home and in exile – a very privileged ministry. His ideas about a 'New Covenant' reached back across the years to the original Mosaic basics of their faith. His concepts towards reform presented ideas of personal trust and faith, replacing failed national responses towards spirituality.

Promise point

No longer could spirituality be a matter for 'other people' within the nation. It was now to be seen as very personal, and individual. The Law would need to be written on every heart. Hope and grace flow through the restoration ideas, replacing old dogmatism. How could the exiles sort out this very new message? In the past, all they had known from Jeremiah seemed like harsh condemnation. Now his voice seemed welcome, and to be offering realistic transition. Were they hearing the same man? Or, for the exiles, was the distance from home helping them to hear more clearly?

Jeremiah and his scribe, Baruch, eventually submitted to enforced exile, not into the midst of the folk they had been writing to, but in the opposite direction – to Egypt, of all places! From there the two men's lives fell into obscurity among others of their countrymen who had sought voluntary residence there.

Their themes were, at least in part, taken up by another of the prophets, Ezekiel. He appears to have been among the exiles prior to the fall of Jerusalem. He was a young married priest who had the classic prophetic ability to go into trances and see visions. A love of dramatic presentation comes through in representations of broken bricks, lying on his side, and baking bread over burning human dung, to mention but a few. His meditation over the present position of exile made him realize that no military credit lay at Babylon's door; this was God's doing, and as punishment upon his people. Sooner or later restoration and forgiveness would be possible. Ezekiel presented a picture of God that was distinctive, almost certainly influenced by being in the different surroundings of Babylon. His vision was no longer curtailed by the homeland's religious confusion. God was to be seen in terms of intense glory and awe-filled majesty, sometimes in terms akin to those in the book of Revelation. 🖙 5 By contrast, humanity, as painted by Ezekiel, was small and insignificant.

The fulfilment and development of Jeremiah's words, now with Ezekiel's ideals, showed their potential in the contrast between the exiled people and the abilities of their captors. Judah's people may have been at a low ebb prior to the exile, but they still had qualities that made them stand out in styles of work and the way they applied themselves. National pride was to remain for many long centuries, and in later history the concepts were to become a significant contribution to lifting spirits once again. But, for now, their reflections on home and the core matters of faith gradually allowed the Law of Moses to assume an importance long forgotten. Stripped

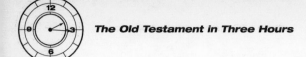
of the temple grandeur, their rites and ceremonies in exile could be practised for their meaning, not for visual impact alone. Keeping the Sabbath and many of their dietary laws came back into daily life, and as a people their resultant distinct style of life began to make a noticeable contrast with those among whom they were forced to live. It is to this period of exilic worship that the idea of the synagogue as a new place in which to worship may have occurred.

Comfort for Exiles

Here in a foreign land the people realized they remained 'chosen' people in the sight of God. One day – yes, one day – they would also discover they were not forgotten. Who would be their deliverer, and when? To this situation there comes the second voice of Isaiah – the voice of the comforter:

> *Comfort, O comfort my people, says your God.*
> *Speak tenderly to Jerusalem, and cry to her*
> *that she has served her term,*
> *that her penalty is paid,*
> *that she has received from the Lord's hand*
> *double for all her sins.*
> Isaiah 40:1–2

Through this prophetic voice comes the message that liberation is on the way. God is about to raise up an international ruler who will surprise even the most optimistic of exiles. The events will be like a motorway journey speeding the return to their homeland. Nothing can stop this happening, just as in days of old nothing could stop the assured flight of the people from Egypt to the Promised Land under Moses. The very presence of God is equally assured and promised in the new journey ahead of them. The second voice of Isaiah – that of consolation – assures the people that God is, and will be, totally in charge of events as they unfold. But before they think future life is going to be the proverbial piece of cake, Isaiah reminds them that they return not just to their homeland but to the covenant relationship with God. Nothing has changed, and the covenant demands remain a partnership obligation. They are still to be a light to the nations of the world, and as a nation to remain 'servant Israel', through whom will come the redemption of all peoples. Within this concept comes a shaft of insight into God's plans through pictures of an 'Ideal Servant'. Were the people to see here pictures of Messiah? Such a concept had been within the original hopes of kingship for the nation, but how tarnished that role had become! Yet, as with so many other things in this phase of life, new thinking was blossoming. 'Ideal Servant', Isaiah had said, and 'anointed one' echoed down their historical memories. A formation time for the full revelation of God was opening up in minds moving out of depression into hope for the future, hope born of an era in which judgement and salvation were being understood. ⌸ 6

Freedom with Fulfilment of Dreams

5 3 8 BC

Cyrus was a Persian king who had taken the leadership and possession of Assyria, Mesopotamia, Syria, Armenia and Cappadocia. He proclaimed himself 'king of the world, great king, legitimate king, king of Babylon, king of Sumer and Akkad, king of the four rims of the earth, son of Cambyses, great king, king of Anshan ...' On and on went his self-elevating titles, and we get the message – he was in charge of what was probably the largest piece of territory ever controlled by a single man in the Middle East. He was at heart a very humane ruler, and on matters of religion gave freedom to all his subjects. That included the Jews, a term which from this point on can be used for the remnant of the Hebrew peoples exiled from Judah.

Upon assuming control of Babylon he issued an edict, which under Medo-Persian law could never be changed. It opened the door to a return to Jerusalem, and to the restoration of God's people to their former lands. Not all wanted to go, for many had created a very acceptable new lifestyle in these foreign lands that they were not prepared to put in jeopardy by returning to a broken-down city and

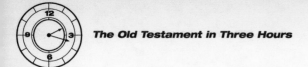

nation, and certainly not to the dangers that would be encountered. Of those who were willing to take the risk, not all wanted to return at once. There is no doubt, however, that the first waves of returning people were impressive, and that historic memories of the first entry into the Promised Land would have been rekindled.

Another excitement was present in the person, among the returning exiles, of Zerubbabel as governor of Jerusalem. Here was a man in direct line of succession to David. The visions of restoration of kingship under the original promises of God were not lost on the community. David had once been the saviour of the people. Was it putting too much into their hopes for the future that this link to the past would also create the right conditions for an imminent salvation, also through a Messiah figure?

Rebuilding

5 3 6 BC

Arduous and dangerous years lay ahead. Right from the start it was difficult for the first people who returned to know just where they stood with the edict, or agreement, that permitted their journey. One version seems to imply that the people were free to return with gifts from their neighbours. Another says that they were also entitled to have partial compensation for the damage done to the nation, with the temple being rebuilt at government expense. Cyrus had plans and specifications drawn up in advance, based on the needs identified by an advance party led by Shesh-bazzar two years earlier. The apparent generosity of Cyrus seems incredible when comparing the numerical insignificance of Judah's exiles with that of the population in his whole expansive empire. What did Cyrus have to gain? To all his people he attempted to grant circumstances that would make them contented. They remained controlled vassals, but at least Cyrus knew he would have their goodwill if Egypt ever tried to create problems for his empire.

There is an element of confusion surrounding the reasons why the temple had to wait twenty years for significant work to be done on it. Were they waiting for that promised funding? There is evidence that Samaritan opposition hindered them, but hostility was only to be expected, just as it was when the first invasion of the Mosaic period burst upon the local residents. What we do know is that some form of significant restoration of worship took place, probably among the ruins, developing the continuity of what had been retained on the site while the exiles had been away, developing and most certainly adding the refreshed ideas of covenant which the exiles had gained. Here were people determined to hold on to their newly restored faith. But was it sufficiently firmly founded in personal commitment? ☕ 7 Only time and testing would tell.

5 2 0 BC

The voice of Haggai entered their experiences. Despite a drought with resultant near-famine conditions hitting the community hard, he sensed that the people cared less concerning rebuilding the temple than they did towards personal comfort. If these were people who had really rediscovered faith, what did they think they were playing at, he challenged.

Three weeks later the impact of his words resulted in noises of hammer and shovel in the temple area. But dispirited people are not easily inspired to maintain effort. Just a few weeks later than that, Haggai was issuing words about the arrival of that hoped-for Messiah, and the riches that would come to his kingdom from all nations. Was this the deliverer they waited for, and is this the time? No. Haggai may have misread the signs, but to him lies the credit for adding his voice to the life of the community which just four years later would have finished the temple.

His was not a lone voice. At the same time Zechariah was another encourager, with a message not just about the temple but on wider issues. He too felt that the time was right for some form of Messiah figure to emerge. His later prophetic oracles (chapters 9 to 14) included people rejoicing at the sight of a king coming gently riding on a donkey.

Rejoice greatly, O daughter of Zion!
Shout aloud, O daughter of Jerusalem!
Lo, your king comes to you;
triumphant and victorious is he,
humble and riding on a donkey,
on a colt, the foal of a donkey.
Zechariah 9:9

He had the glorious vision of the whole world eventually focusing its attention on the Jewish nation and their God.

From here on, the narrative is not easy to follow. Perhaps part of the problem is the splitting of Ezra and Nehemiah from their origins as a single narrative. The compiler of 1 and 2 Chronicles was possibly the editor of these works also. The division causes a great debate as to who arrived among the people first – Ezra or Nehemiah. Ezra was not an official of the Persian court; Nehemiah was. Yet Ezra appeared to arrive with wide authority and powers to stimulate everything that was needed, such sweeping powers that even included virtual open access to the Persian royal treasury. One might have expected such powers to be allocated to Nehemiah.

Applying the Law to Life

Ezra was a priest and a scribe, respected as such within the Jewish law by the Persian authorities. As a priest, he had to face up to a problem of the purity of God's returning people. From the times of Moses they had been warned not to intermarry with foreigners. After many years in exile it is hardly surprising that love knew no barriers and blossomed across national origins. Among the Jews who returned there were 113 mixed marriages. It seems strange that a power-backed Jewish priest could do little more than lament such a situation. 📖 8 Yet in Jewish history Ezra is a man of high respect, held by some religious leaders almost as high as Moses himself. He is pictured as coming home with the Law of God in his hand. That is a picture very reminiscent of Moses the Law-giver. But if Ezra did arrive first, the law was not ratified for nearly a quarter of a century, and then in the presence of Nehemiah.

Some of the apparent difficulty with the period could come about because the two men were of totally different personalities. Ezra seems quiet, almost ineffective. Of his piety and learning there can be no doubt. Nehemiah, on the other hand, comes over as a bold charismatic man of action. The qualities of both these leaders were a vitally important combination across this era of national re-establishment.

In the end it probably matters little about who did what and when. The feel of the age is of a people returning home having rediscovered their faith, but a people for whom the impetus to rebuild more than the basic necessities of life was difficult to hold on to.

Into the general arena of the period comes the voice of Malachi the messenger. The temple may have appeared in the midst of the people, but the visions of Zechariah were far from becoming reality. The messenger saw the people backsliding as a result, and the priesthood losing both sense of direction and its vocation to God. They were bored stiff. 🖵 9 Divorces were happening, along with marriages to foreign girls. He longed for the return of an Elijah-like person so that Messiah could be revealed.

Despite these lapses among the community, the high ideals of faith restored in exile were still the intention of many. Before them were to be times of testing to shake the very fundamentals of a faith grasped but not yet totally integrated into life. The critical words of the prophets about their priorities were heard, plus prophetic visions of Jews and Gentiles alike pouring into their land. That would bring more and more pressure upon them. Then the voices added demands of prayer and worship – how much more were they supposed to cope with? 🖵 10 Most of the people wanted to know why all the words of present hope were not turning themselves into practical realization. Cracks began to appear in religious resolve – voices were heard again asking if God's power was sufficient. Elements began to evolve among the returning exiles of those who wanted to be 'pure' Jews, uncontaminated by the waverers and the impure religion practised by the local residents. It was a feature that was to have both strengths and weaknesses in later history.

Chapter 8 Questionline

There are few people who can go through life holding fast to faith without questions being asked. If answers are not found, faith can too easily evaporate. Questionline looks at some aspects of this period of Jewish history with this possibility in mind.

1 Reflecting on one's own life demands a high degree of integrity and honesty. Under such conditions, making excuses to ourselves for past mistakes is all too easy. But are we really going through this exercise for self? Does God really know what is in our hearts, our thoughts, our very intimate being? The answer to this makes a very big difference to how we carry through such a review.
Bible Notes ✎ *Jeremiah 31:31–4*

2 Was this a move akin to the modern term 'ethnic cleansing'? Probably that would be too strong a term for this short-lived experience. But when excessive nationalistic pressures are put upon a group within any society, which becomes uppermost in people's minds – basic survival or faith? Can faith survive under the pressures of secular society today? How?
Bible Notes ✎ *Daniel 3:19–30*

3 Why is the modern Christian Church so easily thrown into feelings of depression and despair? Falling numbers, loss of the power of the Holy Spirit, financial pressure – what would be on your list? On a personal level, what brings spiritual depression and despair? Should we ever feel like this as people of faith in God?
Personal reflection

4 What is the nature of your calling to serve God? Why were you called to a life of faith and so many of your friends not called? Do we sufficiently often identify the nature and content of our call as individuals, and reappraise what we have done within it?
Bible Notes ✎ *Jeremiah 1:4–19*

⛫ 5 As the Old Testament story unfolds, the character of God reveals itself in changing ways: the majesty and power of a God of creation, through to the punishing persona. Can a relationship be built towards a God of Ezekiel's style of glory and majesty – features that are too far outside the human experience to be approachable?
Bible Notes ✎ *Ezekiel 1:1–28; Revelation 4:1–11*

⛫ 6 In coming to know the God to whom our prayers are offered, it is comforting to be assured that he is the God who saves us from our sins. But that concept is presented alongside the not-so-comfortable idea of judgement. Can the two concepts be held together as we try to know God?
Bible Notes ✎ *Isaiah 43:25–8*

⛫ 7 In the historical scene, the people were moving away from national religion to personal religion. Today, personal religion has eclipsed national religion. Would there be justification for seeking to know God on a national basis as well? Could it be achieved, and how?
Bible Notes ✎ *Ezra 10:1–5*

⛫ 8 The New Testament also taught Christians not to be 'unequally yoked' in marriage. Are we being unfaithful to God to marry non-believers or people of another faith? This principle, carried to extremes, might mean that the loss of faith by a partner would be grounds for divorce. Is this how we are really to act as we come to know the will and nature of the God in whom our faith rests?
Bible Notes ✎ *Ezra 9:1–4*

⛫ 9 How easy it is to be full of religious fervour one moment, but lapsing into passive response in a short period of time. Is our response to God always to be seen as cheerful confidence? Does a passive phase not give us time for reflection?
Bible Notes ✎ *Malachi 2:1–9*

🖰 10 What is our answer to the modern pressurized world when it challenges prayers that go unanswered? When our expressions of hope and trust in God are met by scenes of natural catastrophe? When our confidence in the second coming of Christ awaits fulfilment two thousand years later? Where is the God we proclaim?
Bible Notes ✎ *Nehemiah 13:15–22*

Chapter 8 Bible Search

The fall of Jerusalem	2 Kings 25:1–21; Jeremiah 2:3–30; 2 Chronicles 36:15–21
Ezekiel among the exiles at the Chebar Canal	Ezekiel 1:1; 3:12–21
Exiles involved in profitable activities	Nehemiah 1:11; Isaiah 55:1–2; Zechariah 6:9–11
Exiles defect to the worship of Babylonian deities	Isaiah 46:1, 2, 12; 50:11
The edict of Cyrus allowing Jews to return home from exile	2 Chronicles 36:22–3; Ezra 1:1–4
Calls for the start to rebuilding the temple	Haggai 1:1–15; Ezra 5:1–17

Theme Prayer

Comforting God, my faith can be tested by many things, and too easily I can fall into depression and despair as I look at the world in which I live. Then I remember that this is not my world, but yours. Forgive my weak resolve, and renew my response to your offer of power. Amen.

Chapter 9

Building a Family of Faith

Bible Account
Ezra chapters 7–10
Nehemiah
Isaiah
Ruth
Jonah
Esther
Joel

STORYLINE

What an amazing spectacle is the opening ceremony of any Olympic Games. The colour, the presentation, the fireworks and the grand parade of athletes. No matter which country we live in there is an eager sense of expectation as each flag arrives and we await our own colours. There must be very few of us who carry no sense of nationalism at such a moment. Even within an event where colour or creed should have little meaning, there is still something that wants 'our' team to do well and to build the status of the nation represented.

The Persian Pressure

The families returning to the Jewish homeland had the responsibility of building the status of their nation. What they were involved in was no game: it was a fight for survival. How can you build a nation when you are still the servant of another, and one that holds the control strings of a huge empire? Persia. The simple answer is that – in the main – you can't. ☕ 1

The Persian Empire was a powerful organization, but like all such confederations it had moments when crumbling control systems threw up causes and pressures that could point towards potential total disintegration. A kinsman of Cyrus had to put his personal stamp on the empire in one such moment, resulting in a much stronger control than had previously been possible to visualize. The Jews who had returned to their own land may well have found this an uncomfortable phase of re-establishment – certainly Zerubbabel vanished from the scene around this time, perhaps eliminated by the Persian controllers for apparent rebellion, which may have been no more than trying to establish that important national identity once again against a background of new controls.

The Samaritan peoples living in the land also made trouble. They exercised many complaints against the 'incomers', but the legal document signed by Cyrus could always be produced to stop legal wrangles. 'We have permission, and it can't be changed,' they could claim. But resultant tension was a significant factor in history from this point on, one no court dialogue could remove.

Their security may not have been assured, but a start on the rebuilding of the temple was a trigger for celebration. Singing, shouting; musical instruments of all sorts came out. Some wept – perhaps they could see from the start that the financial and practical resources were never going to be enough to replace what had once stood as a glorious place of worship.

5 1 6 BC

The temple was complete. But the party that had signalled the start of its renewal was out of keeping with the twenty long years of sweat and toil, and the periods of loss of enthusiasm. The events during the next phase of history rely upon the books of Ezra and Nehemiah, but for part of it we need to look to the Apocrypha, and to such historians as Josephus. In the immediate period the walls of the city were made secure against a background of more pressure from the Samaritans bringing from Nehemiah the response of sitting down, weeping, mourning and praying. Crying seemed to be in fashion, Ezra had done the same over the sins of the people, additionally pulling his hair and beard to pieces and tearing his clothes, thus calling attention to his grief, particularly over intermarriage. ⬚ 2

The Torah and its Implications

A conference of all the heads of families from among all the returned exiles created representative involvement of the people in facing up to the religious implications. The Book of the Law of Moses, the Torah, was read to the now settled people, with Ezra standing on a specially constructed platform facing the square by the Water Gate of Jerusalem. Some of the people needed the priests to translate the words. The original language, Hebrew, was difficult for the people, some of whom had been brought up to speak the Aramaic language of Persia. Other people were present, having come from their self-imposed exile in many of the surrounding nations. Not all of them would have spoken Aramaic. As the force and impact of the Law dawned on the gathered people, it was their turn to weep.

What a sight it must have been as the whole gathered congregation then started to rush around like a nest of ants. They were intent on building booths in which to live while, day after day, the whole Law was presented and explained to them. In so doing they were resurrecting features of one of the former great annual festivals linked to the agricultural year. Now it was destined to become a focus for pilgrimage that would eventually draw Jews from far and wide around the Persian Empire – to the delight of highwaymen seeking easy pickings.

For now, atonement for the past was within their realization of how life should be lived under the Law, and the message spread. ⏄ 3 It may seem strange to throw dust and ashes into one's hair, and to change ordinary clothes into itchy sackcloth. It was not meant to be a shampoo, but to show the seriousness of the confession intention of the gathered community. Confession of the whole of past history. And a history they now recognized as littered with failures of religious zeal.

The confession preceded the making of a special binding agreement in writing. The seals of all leaders and priests present were placed on it for good measure. Here were people firmly intent on living a life as God wanted it and avoiding those many past mistakes. They became very protective of their newly discovered zeal, both in worship and in relationships with other people. They were a 'separated' or 'special' and called people; zeal was at the heart of their intentions. The understanding of a covenant relationship with God was probably at its height and as it had never before been comprehended. It was not just the city that had walls surrounding and protecting its inhabitants: their lives were now also encompassed by faith. ⏄ 4

Ezra could at last tackle the problem of illegal marriages – the people could see the point of being a 'pure' nation now. Divorce rates most certainly soared. The people were putting their faith, inseparable from their Law, into practice. But some commentators would argue that the real focus of what was happening was the birth of a self-righteous legalism, rather than true faith and trust in God. ⏄ 5

There are arguments that the strictures of zealous legalism borne of this period were opposed by some. The story of Ruth portrays a section of history much earlier than the return from exile – it tells the story of a family containing mixed marriages, yet despite that at the heart of the story comes Ruth, the great-grandmother of that classic of all kings, David. The story begins with an implication that it was written much later, saying 'In the days when the judges ruled …' Some scholars feel that it was written to protest about the teachings of racial purity imposed on the returning exiles.

Esther is another story written either at the time of Ezra's return or in the period of the Maccabees (see Chapter 10). It's an odd and much argued about book, for there is no mention of God, or the land of Judah, or Jerusalem. However, God is clearly implied as controlling the events. It is of interest at this point in our own story for two reasons. First, contained within it is the background to the origin of one of the important Jewish festivals – Purim. We see Esther, a Jewish lass, being promoted to queen alongside King Xerxes (or Ahasuerus, if you prefer). It is a tale of her attributes over all local Persian people, and of Jewish revenge on those who attempt their downfall. So the second reason for inclusion at this point in our own story is that of Jewish supremacy being strong.

The book of Jonah has some Aramaic expressions within it. The story could be interpreted as protest against isolationist policies. Jonah is portrayed as prepared to go to any lengths rather than share his faith outside self-imposed boundaries. He'd even allow non-Jews to die rather than change his views, and the story carries within it an implication of his assumption that God agreed with his prejudices. In the end he had to change his thinking and repent, allowing the once-wicked foreigners of Nineveh the opportunity for salvation. Such a story, combined with the Aramaic, could point to the tensions in this period of history.

The ideas behind the scholarship of Ruth, Esther and Jonah are representative of the fact that not everyone was carried away by the new-found policy of active religious zeal. There is no event in the whole of history that carries total agreement among any community. However, what is of paramount importance is the fact that the faith of the Jewish people, cut off from the temple in the exile period and thus threatened with permanent obscurity, had returned to the homeland in much better health. What was now born was not just the expected pride in their nation as such, but a much more important emphasis on personal piety and prayer. ⬙ 6 They were people of a new age, with new circumstances, and with pride in the Law which governed life.

The Dawning of Light
The voice from the Isaiah school of thought sounds afresh. No longer are chapters 56–66 concerned with the servant pictures earlier in the

'comfort' writings. The emphasis is on cultic matters very much akin to the period after the exile. The three phases of the Isaiah narrative can be taken to be a changing picture of God relationships – before, during and after the formative period of the exile. Only now, having come through this terrible experience, can the voice of Isaiah call upon the people to arise as within light, promising that the glory of God rises with them, God's redeeming glory is upon them. Yet a note of caution on styles of religious observance can be heard also from Isaiah, who links observance with community responsibility.

> *Is not this the fast that I choose:*
> *to loose the bonds of injustice,*
> *to undo the thongs of the yoke,*
> *to let the oppressed go free,*
> *and to break every yoke?*
> *Is it not to share your bread with the hungry,*
> *and to bring the homeless poor into your house;*
> *when you see the naked, to cover them,*
> *and not to hide yourself from your own kin?*
> Isaiah 58:6–7

The voice is calling to the people, warning that fasting, a feature of legalistic interpretation of worship and practice, may in fact become self-indulgence and promotion. Instead, there needs to be a spirit of social justice, love, compassion, caring and empathy as practical ways of demonstrating true faith. ⬚ 7 If these passages are related to the period after exile, they are sounding a note totally in keeping with the new covenant – the New Testament – rather than any new age generated within the people by and for themselves, in an ivory tower sense of being an exclusive and isolated people of faith.

The voices of warning and the voices of protest were present to guide away from letting religious zeal get out of hand. Yet the fact was, it was vitally important that they did understand the re-establishment of worship and personal prayer, plus appreciation of the Torah. The building of a family of faith was full of tension, full of options and full of potential hazards.

Samaritan Tensions

Can one build a family relationship leaving some members of it isolated or rejected? One of the sad things arising from this period was the antagonism that developed towards the Samaritan people – residents of the area occupied by the northern tribes, but not wholly contained in that geography. Was the difficulty that they were already resident in that area? There had been past tensions between north and south since the times of David. There had also been times of helpful mutual co-operation. It cannot have been just the old rivalries that created the tensions between the returning Jews and the Samaritans. There is no doubt that the Jewish protectionism towards their faith and way of life would have created a barrier. Samaritans would have been looked down upon as having only a thin veneer of understanding of Judaism. Converts would not have been welcome even had they dared to seek greater understanding. ☐ 8

The Samaritans would claim their own rights – that they were the direct descendants of the old northern tribes, who had been taken into exile but who had returned long before the Jews. Their understanding of the rivalry went back into history, and to the times of Eli. There had been a split over where worship should have its focus, claiming their priority view for Mount Gerizim, not Jerusalem, Zion. The work of Ezra and Nehemiah, therefore, in renewing a second place of worship at Jerusalem and making unique claims for it, was viewed by Samaritans as adding insult to original injury. They styled themselves as *Shâmerîm*, 'the observant ones', rather than *Shômerônîm*, meaning 'inhabitants of Samaria', a twist on words that was to have significant tensions for long years of hatred and rivalry.

The period of Jewish resettlement was to be a time of tension, setting boundary demarcation between Samaria and Judah. Geography, worship, religious purity and zeal stood between these parts of what could have been an international family with a degree of common heritage. ☐ 9

335 BC

The division between the two peoples culminated in the erection by

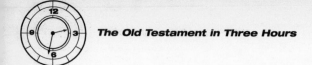

the Samaritans of a rival place of worship to Jerusalem on their sacred Mount Gerizim. The authenticity of the story of a priest from Jerusalem marrying Nicaso, daughter of Sanballat, governor of Samaria, has been questioned. Yet the event, and his refusal to divorce her, has somehow become enshrined into the annals of the building of the Gerizim worship centre. The Samaritans claimed that this focus for their worship existed before creation and escaped the Flood, as it will escape destruction of all things at Doomsday. Such comments and claims were presented to the intense anger of Jews. Samaritans had their views on resurrection to follow the day of 'vengeance and reward' at the end of time, when the earth will split open and the faithful will be robed in clean, sweet-smelling garments. There is some probability that the origins of some Samaritan religious ideas blended Jewish and Islamic ideas, although the exact date of such a blend cannot be ascertained for certain. Whatever the truth behind the origins and developments, there is a very clear and distinct division between their resettlement and that of the unfolding Jewish community that enshrined religion in every part of life.

A Threat on the Horizon

The great power of the Persian Empire left the Jewish people a mixture of restriction and freedom to rebuild life. It was an uncomfortable arrangement, not just to Jews – unable to do much about it – but to other restored peoples as well. The Greeks were rising in power and dominance. They had the strength to do something about it. Alexander III of Macedon, alias Alexander the Great, with the background of Aristotle as a personal tutor, came to his country's throne in a frame of mind which determined to sort out the Persian control. He started a whole series of expeditions, and took much (some would say most) of the old Persian power and lands to himself. His conquests reached out as far as the Indus river in one direction and into north Africa in the other. His troops were no different to their modern counterparts, and enjoyed some of the foreign travel but hated the length of time they were away from home. There are allusions to Alexander in the Bible records of Daniel and Zechariah, and in the Apocrypha in 1 Maccabees. A fever brought his life to an untimely end at the age of only thirty-three.

There are claims that the Jews were treated with preference by Alexander. The picture may be slightly influenced in the historical annals by the fact that the Samaritans rebelled against the new ruling power. There is an element of justification for the view of his leniency towards the Jews, for on one of his journeys Alexander was not just greeted by Jewish priests, but even allowed to worship in the temple.

Here was a man who was an avid reader of the Greek legends and philosophies and brought the great Greek traditions into the lives of the people resident in the lands he conquered. A short while before his death he built a great city in one of the other nations he had acquired, Egypt. Alexandria has forever had prestige. The impact of his short life changed the Middle East beyond recognition, and the Greek influence was now to impress itself on Jewish thinking, and later Christian development and its understanding of God.

Joel is a difficult book of the Bible to slot into historical order. We can't identify either him or his father. Nor does the book contain any historical events to use as dates. He could be as early as the 9th century BC, but many would say he comes into the date range 400 to 350 BC. Some have seen in his depiction of locusts a reference to Babylonians, Medo-Persians, Greeks or Romans. The dating is of less importance than the fact that, under some form of pressure, the call is issued for repentance, on the basis that the day of the Lord is near. He speaks with messages akin to Isaiah, Jeremiah, Amos and Zephaniah, saying that the coming 'day' will bring punishment followed by restoration and blessing, following on from repentance.

Chapter 9 Questionnaire

In building a family of any sort the differences of emphasis in the lives of the different members need to be allowed expression. Members of a family need to 'conform' to an unwritten code in creating harmony, and to share in the resources available fairly and with respect. But beyond that, any inhibition of freedom for personal expression could set up a tension with potential to destroy family unity. Many of these themes are raised throughout this period of history.

🖵 1 Control of other people is a difficult concept. An employer can determine exactly how employees do their work, sometimes at the risk of their losing personal initiative. A parent can, and perhaps ought to, have control over a child. A priest can exercise it over a parish. When are these examples of control constructive, and when destructive?
Bible Notes ✎ Nehemiah 5:14–19

🖵 2 Ezra seems to have had problems of intermarriage as a high-profile matter. But he has it as such a burden that he cries. At other times Nehemiah cries, as does the whole congregation. Crying is an important emotion-releasing mechanism. But it can also be used in family life to gain sympathy, sometimes when it is not due. How appropriate is emotion in the spiritual life?
Bible Notes ✎ Nehemiah 13:23–30; Ezra 9:1–4

🖵 3 A feature of being a family of faith is to acquire the ability to look at past mistakes and to change life accordingly so that a positive view of the future is achieved. Is it easier to acquire this ability on one's own, or among other people? Which features of this ability are easier in community?
Bible Notes ✎ Nehemiah 8:13–18; see Leviticus 23:33–43

🖵 4 Everyone needs to develop a feeling of being secure within their faith towards God: a confidence with God. Can this lead to the danger of feeling that because God is our Father, life's difficulties are somehow by-passed, and will not descend on a person or family of faith?
Bible Notes ✎ Nehemiah chapter 9

🖵 5 The Christian faith has sometimes been accused of restricting people by a set of rules, and even of a form of brain-washed legalism, demanding conformity. How can a community/family of faith avoid becoming self-righteous or legalistic? Or is the faith we proclaim weakened when we avoid 'rules' for its observance?

Bible Notes ✎ *Nehemiah 10:28–39*

⌘ 6 'Piety' is a difficult word in the modern world. How do we define it? Is it appropriate?

Bible Notes ✎ *Ruth 1:6–18*

Personal prayer, for some, is a part of life that needs rediscovery today. The practice in many places is slipping to a point where people need to ask a priest or minister to help them in times of difficulty. How can the importance of personal prayer be encouraged inside the family of faith to a point where these 'skills' can be shared with others?

⌘ 7 The tensions between personal piety and practice in faith and its application within the community have always faced those who want to live a 'religious' life. Too much piety, and we are accused of being so heavenly minded that we are of no earthly use. Too much community work, and we are accused of having a 'social gospel' and as a result have lost touch with God. How, and where, is the balance to be struck?

Bible Notes ✎ *Isaiah 56:1–8*

⌘ 8 Does the Christian Church, perhaps inadvertently, put up the same barriers? Members of the local community often express themselves as fearful of going into a church because they are ignorant of what goes on. They fear breaking into a 'club'. Even the fear of sitting in somebody's favourite seat is a real one for some visitors to a church. In their own way, these folk feel unwelcome among 'experts' in the faith. How can these barriers be broken down?

Personal reflection

⌘ 9 The family of God's people around the world is divided despite years of ecumenical activity. Styles of worship are divisive. Why?

What are we afraid of? Denominations divide. The stance of theology, liberal or evangelical, divides. Too often people of another faith are seen as 'rivals' rather than seekers after one God. How are we to rid ourselves of suspicion, reservation and rivalry, replacing it with respect?

Bible Notes ✎ **Isaiah 57:14–21**

Chapter 9 Bible Search

Ezra pulls his hair out over mixed marriages	Ezra 9:1–4; Zechariah 13:23–31
The Festival of Booths is restored	Nehemiah 8:13–18
Portrayal of mixed marriages	Ruth 1:1–14
Portrayal of Jewish supremacy	Esther 2:1–18
Portrayal of Jewish isolationist ideas	Jonah 1:1–4; 3:1–10

Theme Prayer

Incomparable God, I thank you for faithfulness towards me. I ask for strength to be firm in my commitment. Forgive me for the times I stumble while trying to work out the meaning for my faith in today's world. Help me to find my place in the Christian family, and in your world. Amen.

Chapter 10 Preview

The spread of the Greek Empire, illustrated at the end of Chapter 9 and now to be developed, is of great importance at the close of the Old Testament years. Strictly speaking, we have partly left the Old Testament behind and enter into the history covered by books in the Apocrypha. 'Apocrypha' means 'things that are hidden': quite why such a designation should have been given to them is shrouded in confusion.

For many long years these books were held at arm's length by parts of the Christian tradition. This is because the origins of many of the books were not part of the Hebrew Bible. They were, however, part of the Greek and Latin Bibles from the beginning, and ecumenical ventures like the Revised Standard Version Common Bible and the New Revised Standard Version include them after the Old Testament. The early church Fathers did not hesitate to use them.

Parts of the Apocrypha are expansions on the Old Testament books – for example, there are some fascinating extra Daniel stories. His role as a detective would have Sherlock Holmes envious, and his exploits with a dragon would be the envy of George, the English patron saint. There is more of the wisdom of Solomon, some additions to the Esther stories, and hints of Jeremiah.

The books that are useful in bridging the gap between the Old and New Testaments are those of 1 and 2 Maccabees. This part of history contains struggles, battles and tensions as Greek, Roman and Jewish ideas clashed. The purity of the Jewish faith received military protection by zealous Jews.

As the Greek influence spread, so the Old Testament became translated into that language. For modern readers the Old Testament appears as a single unit of pre-Christian literature, carefully subdivided into types of documents, rather than attempting historical chronology. They actually began life as separate scrolls. Copies of other scrolls were easily added to them as they lay in libraries of important documents. As the work of Greek translation proceeded, little attempt was thought necessary to distinguish between authenticity and value. To Greeks, all learning had intrinsic value. The important point is that the Apocryphal books were written in Greek, probably because Jews in Alexandria, and possibly also in Antioch, spoke Greek in preference to Hebrew or Aramaic.

The Importance of the Period for Christians

It is right for Christians to try and appreciate the difficult days that led up to God's chosen solution for all humanity. It is right to discover that in this period came the dawning of an important theological teaching, the resurrection of the dead. It has been alluded to in the opening verses of Daniel 12 and is now to be made explicit in 2 Maccabees 7. The New Testament writers and church members also drew foundational strength from the concept when faced with the teachings of Christ, and his resurrection.

The spread of Greek influence was, therefore, not just by military might and empire creation, but, as Chapter 10 will reveal, also in matters of literature and theological reflection.

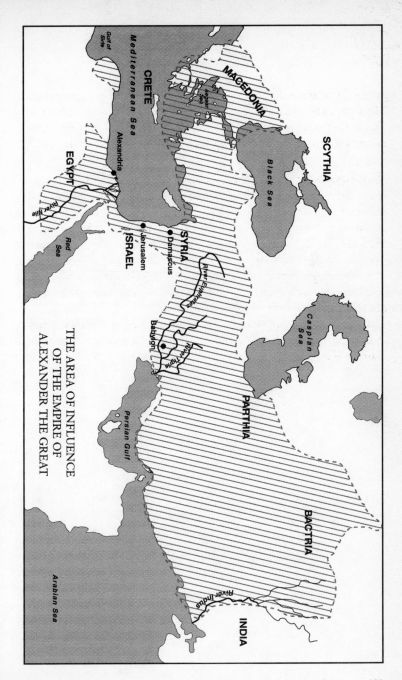

THE AREA OF INFLUENCE
OF THE EMPIRE OF
ALEXANDER THE GREAT

Mediterranean Sea

CRETE

Gulf of Sirte

EGYPT

River Nile

Alexandria

Red Sea

Jerusalem

Damascus

ISRAEL

SYRIA

River Euphrates

River Tigris

Babylon

Persian Gulf

Arabian Sea

River Indus

INDIA

BACTRIA

PARTHIA

Caspian Sea

Black Sea

SCYTHIA

MACEDONIA

Aegean Sea

Chapter 10

Zeal for God

Bible Account
1 Maccabees
2 Maccabees
Daniel
Esther

STORYLINE

Alexander the Great had been a fantastic leader of his men. In around ten years the Middle Eastern scene had changed from one controlling domination to another. Fortunately for the Jews, the new regime was to one that continued to favour their freedom of religious expression. On paper, that is. For Alexander was not just a military man: he was also prepared to share his academic standing and his enthusiasm for all things Greek. He had a vision that if the world could be united under one language and one philosophical approach, it would be a much better place. He was not alone in that view, and the superiority of Greek language and culture was promoted with the enthusiasm of modern advertising executives.

When Alexander met his untimely death the empire he had created was subjected to a power struggle, with four generals each striving to claim the crown. The result was division containing two power sources of significance to the Jews. One was based in Egypt: the Ptolemies. They were matched by the Seleucids controlling Syria and

Mesopotamia. The two groups were to take the Jews back into their historical problems of once again sitting, geographically, between rival power blocs. It had been uncomfortable before, and was to be even worse this time.

Initially, control of their life was in the hands of the Ptolemies. It didn't feel too bad, because they showed respect to the Jewish faith. In fact, the number of Jews living in Egypt grew significantly. This may have been as a result of a new enforced exile, but later, after freedom had been granted, many opted to remain where they were. How history repeats itself! The records of that period show that Jews in Egypt were allowed to retain 'the laws of their fathers', to have their own leaders and to build synagogues. Alexandria had a particularly strong community of Jews. A combining of Jewish and Greek ideas that was to be influential took place there, flowing back into the homeland and wherever Jews lived under the Greek philosophies. It was almost certainly here that the Jewish scrolls started to appear in the Greek language. These were invaluable, as many Jews were now growing up speaking Greek, sometimes with greater fluency than Hebrew.

At home, Jerusalem grew in strength and in population, even after allowing for further emigration to other lands.

3 1 5 BC

Ptolemy held control for only a short time before Antigonus displaced him, only to be pushed aside himself in a battle, and Ptolemy was again in charge. Not for long; just a few years later the two again changed places. In 301 BC the matter was finally settled in a battle at Ipsus with the death of Antigonus. But that did not bring peace. The Jews must have realized with some fear that the settlement of that internal struggle in Egypt had triggered a bigger potential uprising between the Ptolemies and the Seleucids.

After years of unrest the Seleucids, under Antiochus the Great, took control of the Jews along with all the other inhabitants of Palestine. Perhaps now there could be peace, and the civil and religious life of the Jews could settle to some form of normality. As

Alexander had created his own Greek city in Egypt, so now the Seleucids began a whole series of their own. One line of them ran down the Mediterranean coast. The Greek pattern of life was strengthening, and through these cities educational programmes were made available, reaching out to all sections and ages of the community around them, with a particular emphasis on youth. These contacts with local populations brought enhanced appreciation of Greek art and culture, including the theatre. Young people got caught up in wearing the latest trendy clothing to show their participation in the mind-opening opportunities. They could show the modern teenager a lead – apart, that is, from the sprouting of mobile phones!

Jewish parents looked on with the same growing unease as they do today. Infiltrating within the new ideas were pseudo-religious practices. The stress on athletics, for example, led young people into immoral activity. Alarm bells rang in the minds of those who wished to maintain Jewish purity. This was exactly one of those subjects which had left the national faith open to criticism long years before, and which had been part of the national downfall.

| 1 | 9 | 2 | BC

Antiochus may have been victorious once, but a new and even more menacing threat loomed over his domain. In part it was financial. The only way he could solve that was by stealing treasures from worship centres, including Jerusalem. Another threat hanging over him was far more serious than internal accountancy. The Roman armies had been on the move for quite a while, and regarded his alliances with Egypt and Syria with great seriousness. Had the alliances been left to consolidate, the growing power of Rome could have been curtailed. Gathering their military power together they menaced his position, and in the Battle of Magnesia crushed the forces available to Antiochus. There followed more power struggles, and the period forms the background to Daniel chapter 11. Greek and Roman influences were now jointly pressing hard on Jewish life and religion. As a result dark clouds of uncertainty hung over their nation, with resultant impact upon their faith.

1 7 5 BC

The name Antiochus Epiphanes means 'God made manifest'. The sense by which the true Jews would shudder to hear it can be readily understood. He was a Seleucid ruler who, seeing his empire losing influence, tried to change things in favour of Greek practices. What happened was an opening up of class divisions. By this time much of the Jewish aristocracy had adopted Greek patterns of life and thought. Not the working classes, who were furious not just at that title adopted by Antiochus, but at the whole attitudes and changes being forced upon them. While the divisions in society were not totally along class structures, tensions were beginning to open up towards major problems for the Jews. Stress mounted among the population against the Romans, the Greeks, their rulers, the aristocracy, against culture, against just about everything. One small spark would set these seething tensions alight.

Antiochus had been snubbed by the Romans and returned to Jerusalem, planning his arrival for a Sabbath day, being sure that the Jews would be too busy with their worship to oppose his actions. His troops entered the city and torched it, taking and killing many of the people. So bad was the damage that he was forced to build his own citadel, Akra, where the troops and Jewish people sympathetic to the Greeks took refuge.

Control of the Jews became fierce. The temple had been desecrated, the people taxed so heavily that they took little persuasion to leave the city to the foreigners. While the policy of Antiochus had been mainly political, he broadened his control by direct attack on religion from this point onwards. Jews were now forced to live the Greek way, not according to their own Mosaic Law. The things which had made the Jewish people distinct, and to which they had witnessed since the times of the exile, were banished. Sacrifices were prohibited, copies of the Law destroyed. The seething fury among the population was building to an inevitable climax.

Then, in December 167 BC, the temple in Jerusalem was found to have been infiltrated by an image of a bearded Greek god, attributed by some scholars as Zeus. The flesh of an animal unclean according to Jewish Law – a pig – was offered in sacrifice before it. The phrase

in the book of Daniel, 'the abomination that makes desolate', relates to this incident. The whole scene was surrounded with ceremonies akin to drunkenness and blatant sexual orgies.

The Jews were not alone in being treated like this. The Samaritan temple on Mount Gerizim suffered the same fate, and the same possible dedication to Zeus.

Where were the religious leaders? Where were those who should have led the worship according to the Law of Moses? Where was anyone of authority and position? All had limply given themselves over to the Greek infiltration. When families began to be slaughtered for refusing to pay homage to an idol in Jerusalem, the final moment of crisis had arrived.

Bloody Revolution

If these foreigners were determined to stamp out Jewish religion, there were those whose seething discontent was ready to resort to armed intervention: the zealots, people with a radical, even warlike, inner tension and rebellion in protecting and expressing the wrath of God. Some scholars use the title 'Zealot', seeing in this period the birth of organized rebellion that would come to its peak in the revolt against Rome around AD 70. Others see in this period 'zealous people'.

Among those who had fled Jerusalem (but not too far) were John, Simon, Judas, Eleazar and Jonathan, the sons of an old priest by the name of Mattathias. The bully-boys of Antiochus entered their village, demanding allegiance to the new worship patterns. Mattathias was looked to as the leader, and the local people watched to see if he would yield to promised enticements and do as he was instructed. He refused, despite temptations that his sons would have an assured future. One Jew came forward with the required heathen sacrifice. Did that person intend to defuse the situation? There was no time to find out as Mattathias lashed out and slew him on the altar prepared for the foul acts of sacrifice.

The moment of rebellion had come. He could not stop now. A Syrian officer stood too close: he too received the same treatment, and the zeal towards the true Law of Moses poured out as the altar

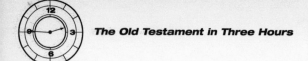

was smashed. In scenes reminiscent of the early life of David, Mattathias fled for his life, taking his sons and a whole band of sympathizers with him. They too fled to the wilderness, as David had done. From that moment on there was no turning back. As more and more brutality was heaped upon faithful Jewish believers, so the zealous inner indignation also grew. The powder keg of rebellion had exploded, but its full force was as yet unspent.

The rebel cause was joined, and numerically greatly increased, by the presence and support of the Hasidim, or Hasidaeans. If the Jewish rebels were full of zeal, the Hasidim showed them how to double it! From now on the whole group were prepared to die for the cause of religious freedom. Their life was based on piety, and there is a possibility that the Dead Sea Scrolls, which so profoundly improved understanding of the original texts of scriptures in the last fifty years of the twentieth century, make direct reference to these pious military giants.

England from 1649 to 1660 was a republic. The words 'Commonwealth' and 'Protectorate' became familiar to the lips of the population. The monarchy was abolished. The House of Lords was abolished. The Anglican Church went with them. Parliament was a hit and miss affair. State assets were sold off to pay for army conquests. The smashing of many works of art took place, and worship deemed to be offensive to the new 'puritan' zeal was radically changed. The Lord Protector was Oliver Cromwell. He pictured himself involved in a crusade akin to that of Moses leading the Israelites from bondage into a new and better style of life. With the benefit of hindsight we might recognize this period of the rise of English zeal as akin to the intertestamental period. Like Cromwell's men, Israel's zealots began to make incursions into their homeland. Judas, son of Mattathias, took control on the death of his father and quickly got the nickname 'Maccabee' ('Hammerhead') to describe his style of leadership.

 BC

Judas Maccabaeus developed the scene from personal rebellion,

through guerrilla tactics, into full battles, and as his reputation grew so did the numbers of those serving with and under him. This was a religious crusade that could not be stopped. The events which followed meant that much blood was spilt. So effective was the crusade that the Jews could again practise their faith, and there is evidence that the zealots came close to their own form of enforcement tactics! Defiance was at its peak. And time and time again military invaders were pushed out of Israel, until at last they were crushed.

Oh that they could get into fortified Jerusalem, and to the centre of all worship! But Syrian troops were stationed there. So great was the zeal that even that difficult objective was achieved, and the desecrated altar torn down and replaced. The great Feast of Dedication (in Hebrew, Hanukkah) became an annual remembrance of this poignant moment of history, beginning on 25th Kislev (December) each year.

Religious Liberty

Freedom may have been obtained for worship in the homeland, but Jews elsewhere were still bound by the Greek overlay of philosophy. Judas Maccabaeus and his brothers set about a policy of invasions to ensure all Jews had the same liberty. It is hardly surprising that both at home and abroad not everyone agreed with their actions. Not everyone sees Cromwell in the same light. One group of Jews who liked the Greek ideas had successfully pleaded for help from outside the nation; for a brief period a Syrian army marched against Judas Maccabaeus, and retreat was the only solution for Judas. Politics forced that Syrian army to withdraw to its base, but Judas had lost control of the prized area around the temple. Syrian rule continued, but religious freedom moved forward one further step with the removal from the country of all traces of the god Zeus. Physical peace reigned over the land. At last!

New Political Visions

What makes up that elusive quality called peace? It is not just the absence of war. Tension remained, because the Syrians, along with

the Greek sympathizing Jews (Hellenizers) were hardly likely to suddenly trust Judas Maccabaeus. They put in a new high priest with Hellenizing views, to protect their position. The adjustments in life necessary after such a radical period of adaptation were many. The support of the Hasidim faded, as their prime goal of religious independence had now been achieved. Military skirmishes broke out from time to time, but did not last.

Judas realized his vulnerability in the new set of circumstances, and opted to seek a friendship alliance with Rome. His aim was to place his land within a power bloc that would balance the military aspirations of other nations who might have devious plans towards him. The treaty was achieved, but the objective backfired. Seeing its potential, Syria sent a huge army, and in the battle many of the followers of Judas fled in fear and Judas was killed. The Hellenizers were quick to grasp their opportunity for control, although religious freedom remained assured. Jonathan, brother of Judas, was elected the new leader of the now hiding band of zealots.

1 5 0 BC

A relative peace had held for some years. The swinging pendulum of control remained, basically, with the Hellenizers. The wall in the temple Mount, keeping Gentiles in their proper restricted place, had been torn down, to the annoyance of the Jewish purists and the nationalist party in the community. Jonathan could move his seat of power to a point just seven miles outside Jerusalem, from where he could – by popular acclaim – begin to judge the people and punish the Hellenizers, and from this point on his power and influence expanded. He came under intense pressure to align himself with competing external powers, while at home he now had a sufficiently secure power base to move into Jerusalem itself.

The external forces were always trying to outbid each other for his favour, one even offering him a gift not theirs to bestow – the role of high priest. Jonathan took it but, as a shrewd diplomat, kept the whole international and home situation in careful perspective. What he also had showered on him was the Syrian gift of Governor

General of Judaea and an assurance of their king's friendship. The total independence of his homeland was now within his grasp, provided nothing swung the politico-religious pendulum again in Israel. The international situation courted him with equal strength from Syria and Rome.

An army rebellion struck at the heart of Syrian power. Taking advantage of it Jonathan further expanded his influence; with his brother Simon he now began to control a much wider area, and could dictate life southwards as far as the borders of Egypt. All appeared to be going well.

Without any warning, an upstart by the name of Trypho took the Syrian throne, and in his heart was a suspicion that Jonathan was capable of unseating him. Under the guise of a friendly invitation to join him in Bethshan, Trypho killed Jonathan's accompanying troops and imprisoned him.

The consternation at losing their leader threw the Jews into turmoil, but quick-thinking Simon stepped into the breach, trying to negotiate a ransom for his brother. Time and time again Trypho reneged on promises, eventually setting out for Jerusalem with his army, leaving behind instructions that Jonathan was to be killed. The alliances Jonathan had forged swung into action and Trypho was dislodged, and committed suicide. But the plans for Jonathan's release could not be made operational quickly enough, and he was killed.

The Maccabean brothers had by this time each built on the gifts and skills of the others. Judas, in his time as leader, had gained religious freedom. Jonathan had added his role as controller of all Judaea. Simon could add to these the final 'jewel in the crown' of complete independence. The unrest left behind by those recent international events meant that Simon was in a position to bang the table with demands, and under a new Syrian ruler, Simon's land, Israel, was granted full recognition and independence.

The times of Gentile control were over. Simon was high priest, and with their power support removed, the Hellenizers were slowly reduced to historical interest. The period of the Maccabee brothers had been a bloodbath of fighting, internally and internationally. It had taken its toll on Israel, but had achieved the objectives idealized

by a significant faction within the earlier exiles on returning to their own land. It was now under their own control, with religious ideals paramount. All was well. Secure. Firm. Or was it?

Reflecting over the period thus far shows that the gains were achieved by a group led by the one family, a group with zealous objectives that would not receive the concurrence of everyone. Many, in their hearts, had deep-seated doubts. Zeal is something that had on previous occasions gone 'over the top' in national history, only to lead to different problems later.

The Hellenists were no longer an organized party within life, but the Greek influence had not left the life of the nation. It was strong throughout many nations around them, and they could not buck the trend. They had to trade with other nations in a style and manner internationally recognized – the Greek system.

Simon was a wise man who amassed great riches. He was a wonderful benefactor, and by fitting out the new army himself was acting just as a Greek ruler would do. He was a pious man of peace. But those who were to follow him did not have his generosity, and the family name was to be dragged down in popular esteem during the years that followed. The situation was far from secure.

Was it a moment of overenthusiasm that changed for ever the appointment of a high priest? It was understandable that a commemoration to the work of the Maccabean family would be set up in the temple in Jerusalem, but it indicated that the high-priestly role would be held by them with hereditary rights, and this by a council decision. While it was fair that the Syrians no longer had a say in choosing the high priest, that did not mean that the decisions and opinions of the people should also no longer have any influence.

130 BC

John Hyrcanus, Simon's third son, took the role of high priest from his father after a short burst of international fighting and intrigue. He immediately ran into major problems as the Syrians attacked Jerusalem. Would they never rest? Over the next twenty years Hyrcanus enjoyed the support of Rome in keeping the Syrians in check, while enjoying a few battles of his own against the Greeks. He would sometimes use foreign troops, paying them out of the proceeds of looting the tomb of King David – hardly something that would gain popular support from among his own people. There are threads running through the historical accounts at this point that he may have had ideas of becoming a Greek-style ruler. He certainly minted coins with his name on one side as high priest, but with Greek fertility symbols on the back.

It was during this period that the names 'Pharisees' and 'Sadducees' became recognized. Hyrcanus could not make up his mind which of the two groups he supported. Tension started to arise from within these religious groups to challenge his right to hold the office of high priest. The dangers of mixing political ambition and reaching out for secular power were all too clear in the manner and style of Hyrcanus.

In the Pharisees there was a resurgence of an old idea going back to the time of Ezra. During the exile the people, without a place of worship, had focused their minds on the Law, and from that point on it had become a focal point to a continuing and significant body of people, who were now to become known as Pharisees. Close beside them were the experts on the Law, the Scribes or 'Doctors of Law'. Throughout the Maccabean period there had been priestly and lay experts struggling to maintain the Law, and some were now to emerge as a distinct group in society.

The Sadducees had their focus on the temple rather than the Law, and on the role of the priesthood. They were in the main from the aristocratic wing of society. To quite a marked extent the priests had gone through stages of accepting infiltrated Greek ideas. The Sadducees were not to be so acquiescent towards another set of imposed ideas that was just around the historical corner for them, and for the whole nation: those of the Romans.

| | 6 | 3 | BC |

The ever-expanding Roman Empire had points of military vulnerability. One was in the whole area to the east of Israel. It had become the Roman Province of Syria, and was the line of defence against the repeated invasions of the Parthians. Israel itself had come under Roman control, but some parts of it remained self-governing. Yet little by little the centralization of control moved towards Rome, involving even appointments to the role of high priest. That rankled very considerably with the Pharisees, but they in turn became persecuted people, some of their number suffering crucifixion. That was a punishment long used by the Phoenicians and Persians. It was a public method of execution that would bring shame on the transgressor as they hung on a cross, sometimes for days at a time. Under Roman law now impacting into public life in Israel, it was normally reserved for non-Romans as a form of ultimate punishment. Whenever it was used in Israel, it served as a powerful reminder that the people were living under the control of a foreign power. In the light of all that had gone on in recent history, the loss of national sovereignty symbolized in such a brutal way was yet another cause of the discontent that was again coming to the boil.

The Roman civil wars were to create a great disturbance in the whole Middle East – struggles for power, the grasping for control and titles. In Israel, Herod had come to the forefront demanding, and obtaining, the agreement of Rome to his use of the title 'King'. It is doubtful if he would have got away with this in times of quieter, therefore stronger, Roman control. He was a skilful man, manoeuvring his way around different implications of the Roman unrest, managing to continue in office until 4 BC.

He was not a ruler the population loved. Yet ironically he probably served and protected Israel in ways other rulers would not have done. The country was, at least in part, protected from the impact of Roman unrest, although the fear of it was not lost on the community.

On a personal level he was to be greatly feared. Ruthless cruelty was showered on those around him; even his own family were not spared.

The strands of tension in Israel were many. That hard-won religious independence was under threat once again. National integrity had been all but lost. The Greek influences, while controlled, would not go away. Groups within society strove for political supremacy. The cherished idea of being a special, separate and chosen people under a covenant with God was again being swamped by new groups promoting the Law. Others wanted to revert to the old supremacy of the temple as the place of residence for Yahweh. Military domination held these whole strands within society under rigid control. Sooner or later something major had to happen. It had done so before in history. Some prayed for intervention once again. But from which quarter and which power bloc this time? Those of religious persuasion longed for God to intervene. But how had their concepts of the 'personality of God' changed over these recent years of unrest?

Some wanted zealous uprisings to go on. To those more passive in faith expression, God's intervention was the only solution to a situation everyone agreed was fast spiralling out of control, and which had all the ingredients of throwing the internal life of the nation back into similar turmoils to those that had led to exile. The threatening clouds rolled over the nation, and few could see any silver lining.

Chapter 10 Questionline

This chapter departs from the usual style of drawing a series of questions out of the text of the story. It concentrates on one topic.

This period was one that contained a long saga of mixing together aggression and strong adherence to matters of faith. It is a subject that has created problems for most of the world religions at some point. To this day, some expressions of faith actively encourage their believers to support aggression as part of mission.

The Christian faith is expressed in different ways around the world, responding to the conditions of life in which faith needs to live and breathe. It is passive in some nations, but resisting oppression in others.

At what point does resistance to wrongdoing, oppression, social injustice, dictatorships and the like entitle a person of faith to take up arms? What is the place of passive resistance? Do we believe that our rulers are appointed by God: if so, are we entitled to resist at all? How do people of faith cope with a ruler who has come to power by usurping the role of an elected person?

St Augustine of Hippo wrote a 22-volume treatise called *City of God* which arose out of the fall of Rome in AD 410. He made a case that the meaning of history is never about the rise and fall of empires or nations. It is all about the 'City of God' on earth.

Down through the centuries, guidelines have been devised to decide which actions can be regarded as a 'just war', and which cannot. Which of the following are relevant today?

1 It must be fought on the authority of the ruler (N.B. not just a military commander).
2 The cause must be just.
3 Those who fight must have a right intention, notably the advancement of good and the avoidance of evil.
4 The war must be fought by proper means.

and to these, three more considerations are quoted by moralists:

5 The war must be a last resort, all peaceful attempts at solution having failed.
6 The war must offer the possibility that the good achieved will outweigh the evils the war will involve.
7 The war must be fought only where there is a reasonable hope that justice will be victorious.

Are some of these concepts outmoded?

Would a person of faith accept the moralist additions? If not, what would replace them?

How would these be changed if one were facing participation in a revolution instead of war? Is there a difference?

How does 'civil strife' differ from war, and revolution?

Bible Notes ✎ Matthew 5:43–8; Psalm 133; Exodus 23:1–9

Chapter 10 Bible Search

Because these are bloodbath times, the range of readings is curtailed to useful essential pictures. Sight must not be lost of the fact that these were also formative times in the understanding of faith and of the nature and person of God, particularly of how he might be understood in times of physical danger.

temple desecrated by Antiochus	2 Maccabees 6:2–4; 1 Maccabees 1:54
Faith holds in the face of torture and death	2 Maccabees chapter 7
Judas Maccabaeus summons to the faithful	2 Maccabees 8:1–9
temple recovered and purified	2 Maccabees 10:1–9

Theme Prayer

Forgiving God, draw close to me. I do harbour grudges and ill will. I am greedy towards my own protection. I am selfish. Renew me with your all-surrounding love. Change me, so that my nature may accord more nearly to your own, and to that seen in Christ, my Lord. Amen.

Chapter 11

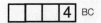

Target minutes used

The Solution?

Bible Account
Matthew chapters 1 and 2
Luke chapters 1 and 2

STORYLINE

| | | | | 4 | BC |

Confusion, suppression, domination and yearnings for the old days were the order of the day. The longing for 'something' to happen to bring them a sense of salvation and restoration was high.

Some wise men sensed 'something' special from signs in the sky.

Some shepherds sensed 'something' special from a disturbed night caring for the flocks.

Months before, a young girl had sensed 'something' special from the unexpected pregnancy developing within her.

A caring husband sensed 'something' special from his young bride-to-be.

A cousin had sensed 'something' special by virtue of the miracle within her womb also.

The sense of threat remained over everyone, and yet ... and yet to an old priest the 'something' was interlinked with his devotion and faith. His vision left him speechless. 'How will I know?' were words that yearned to be spoken.

'How can these things be?' were words that came to the bride-to-be.
Slowly the puzzles in the minds of the family cleared.
The confusion in the community remained.

The drama of God's action, once and for all time to satisfy the needs and aspirations of more than one nation, of all of humanity, came pouring out.

Welcome, little baby, born in a smelly, stinking stable.

Few noticed. In the troubles of the nation, few cared. Few rejoiced. Few understood. ♉ 1

Chapter 11 Questionnaire

♉ 1 In the confused state of the modern world, do we understand any better than the wider community did then?

For God so loved the world that he gave his only son, so that everyone who believes in him may not perish but may have eternal life. Indeed, God did not send the Son into the world to condemn the world, but in order that the world might be saved through him.

John 3:16–17

Chapter 11 Bible Search

Death of Christ	John 19:14–30
Resurrection of Christ	John 20:1–18
Glory of Christ	Acts 1:6–11
Empowerment given for all time	Acts 2:1–13

Theme Prayer

Father God, you have spoken to humanity through times that must have felt like failure and through times of renewal. And now you speak through the gift of a small child. A child destined to be the Saviour of humankind. Help me to listen to you in him. Help me to share the good news. Amen.

Chapter 12

Concepts of God and the New Testament

BEYOND STORYLINE

The Concept of 'God'

There is nothing more annoying than flies on the windscreen when you are driving a car. It seems that, after you have stopped to wash the screen, just a few yards down the road another little fly is hovering, waiting to commit suicide. The irritation comes not in the mess but the place on the screen they choose to splosh themselves. Exactly where the driver looks out. And no matter how hard you try to ignore the mark, the eyes are drawn off the road to focus on the nearer object.

What the Old Testament does is to focus our spiritual vision. We cannot come to the fullness of the Gospels without understanding how the focus of humanity has had the opportunity to change in the centuries that led to the climax of the opening of the New Testament.

As the Old Testament story has progressed, the understanding of God has developed along with it. As the very earliest expressions were first written down during the period of King David, in Psalms for example, through to the exile, so ideas developed. It was during the exile that recollections of history became important enough to record. Alongside this came a dawning new realization of the concept of God.

In creation was God. He was the power of creation, including humanity. God is someone over mankind, disciplining and to be feared because he has the power to change life. Alongside this accurate scene of power came another: how that power was to be exercised. All that mankind could do, realizing vulnerability, was a pathetic fig-leaf protective covering (Genesis 3:7). The power of God was seen in offering more than humanity could possibly do for itself: 'God made garments of skin for Adam and his wife and clothed them' (Genesis 3:21). Before they were banished from the Garden of Luxury, Eden, to fend for themselves, God's power was exercised in loving provision for their protection, and thus for their ultimate salvation.

The surrounding arms of God are seen in the formation of a nation, against all the odds that nature could throw at them, and against a background of servitude to other human beings. Through it all came a new picture of salvation.

The struggle to discern the nature of God was very real as the new nation settled to the task of transition from nomadic to residential styles of living. They mistook features of other religions in the search for truth. It confused the understanding of God. The introduction of kingship to lead the nation had the potential of a figurehead to reveal the person of God through his actions and words. Too often that leadership failed, and the understanding of God went downhill with it.

Prophetic voices warned, trying hard to present fresh concepts of God. But in the main the people concentrated their attention on what seemed more pressing international and local issues.

Life fell apart, and they all but crashed into oblivion as a nation. But again came restoration and salvation, not just to their original land, but also to the power of faith in God.

As they strove to maintain religious zeal there were times of mountain-top style achievement, and moments of slipping back into the valley of despair. But the initiative was God's to raise up people of power in their midst: prophets, priests or even military leaders. The potential of salvation remained even when human determination failed.

In their experience of personal vulnerability, wilderness vulnerability or exile vulnerability, time and time again God could have been seen as punishing and wrathful. That is how he was mistakenly understood for too much of the history. What the story of Israel speaks of, however, is the fact that only by going through wilderness-type experiences or being in the dark valley of life could the people move their understanding of the nature of God forward.

> *Even though I walk through the darkest valley, I fear no evil;*
> *for you are with me; your rod and your staff – they comfort me.*
> *... Only goodness and kindness shall follow me all the days*
> *of my life.*
>
> (Psalm 23:4, 6, including NRSV footnotes)

Time and time again as the history has unfolded we have seen that while God is the Judge of all, he is a judge who takes upon himself the role of reconciliation and restoration, of opening doors to renewed opportunity. The idea of grace comes to the foreground, forgiveness when it is not deserved. God is making a level motorway, or pathway, so that access to him and to his purposes for human life is reachable by all, even those who are self-critical that they constantly fail.

The detailed way in which God initiated dialogue with his people is reflected in special moments of commitment by the Creator, flagged in the story text as seven promises.

Promise points

The importance of them can now be reflected upon at leisure.

1 Through Noah's experiences, God promises to all humankind never to destroy life by flood. What response is called for from humanity? None!
Genesis 9:8–17

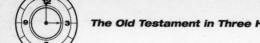

2 Through Abraham's righteousness, God promised the precious gift of land. But God went further and offered it to his descendants as well. What response did God require from him and the family? None!
Genesis 15:9–21; Hebrews 11:8–10

3 Again through Abraham and his household, God promised always to be their God. This time a commitment was called for – devotion, symbolized for them by circumcision to serve as an identity marker linking the people to their God.
Genesis 17:1–14

4 To the whole Hebrew people as they formed into a nation, God promised (covenanted) to be the nation's God for the whole of their future life. What was the response called for? Devotion and service.
Exodus chapters 19–24

5 To Israel was promised the gift of a priesthood for all time, through the priest Phinehas, who had been a man of devotion. The covenant was one of peace, because he had made atonement for the people's sins. What was the response called for? None!
Numbers 25:10–31; see also Psalm 106:30–31; 1 Maccabees 2:26, 54

6 To Israel, through King David, God promised to provide a king for all time from his descendants, capable of making the Promised Land fulfil the potential God had for it. This covenant pointed the way forward to stability for the people because it did away with the need for a power struggle each time a king died. The response demanded of the people? None!
2 Samuel 7:5–16; 1 Kings 4:20–21; 5:3–4; 1 Chronicles 17:1–15

7 The promise was given to Israel in rebellion, through Jeremiah, that while they would lose their Promised Land, they would also

receive, and maintain, forgiveness and renewal of relationships. Response called for? None!

Jeremiah 31:31–4

Instead of 'promise', the word 'covenant' could have been used for an agreement between God and humankind. The Hebrew word means 'bond'. There are many other instances of 'covenant' relationships between God and his people, but these are the core seven accepted by most scholars.

What they illustrate is that God binds himself to his people in terms which either demonstrate his recognition of existing fidelity or which invite devotion responses from people.

These are the concepts of God that forcefully proclaim themselves in the Old Testament story. These are concepts of God that are not limited to the Old Testament but are fulfilled in the New Covenant, and on into the heights, and depths, of modern living. God is as ready now with solutions to cover our 'nakedness' with the wrappings of pre-prepared love as he was from the beginning of creation.

The Old Testament invites every reader not to focus on the wide perspectives of mankind's evil and wrongdoing. Instead, the unfolding story forces everyone who 'drives' their life to keep their eyes focused on a more important point which is, as it were, on the windscreen and so much nearer to themselves. God. And his love-providing salvation. What might be a dangerous change of focus when driving a car is the solution to life as it was meant to be from the beginning, and will be until eternity becomes reality.

New Testament Concepts

It seems like stating the obvious. Yet this book would fail in its objective to be 'basic' if the obvious things were not presented.

The New Testament characters didn't have a Bible. They did have access to the Old Testament. The unfolding story of the climax to the Old Testament in the Apocrypha has revealed how the Old Testament began to appear in Greek.

Christ was well versed in the Old Testament. Time and time

again he would quote passages, to be followed by words such as 'but I say unto you ...' Christ drew also on the teachings of the experts in the Law, and challenged them with their own words. This radical nature of the ministry of Our Lord is only understandable against the Old Testament and the international situation of its time.

The same applies to the work of the apostles. They too had the same resources as they began to establish the Church and as they began to work out a revised understanding of God – theology.

Understanding the impact of the New Testament story can only come into focus through an appreciation of how the people of God got into the difficult and testing situation of their time. Modern understanding and faith must have its foundations there, and can only develop through appreciation of how the New Testament writers gained, and expressed, their appreciation of God.

The story cannot stop with the birth of Christ. The story rolls on and now incorporates every one of us in the enveloping love of a God who did care, went on caring, and invites humankind to respond.

Acknowledgements

There are many people who deserve thanks for their encouragement in the production of this book. To my late wife, Evelyn, I dedicate it, for it was her loving insistence that made sure I kept my promise to Haywards Heath United Reformed Church and put our experiment in storytelling into print. Her long resisting fight with cancer meant that she saw only the first few chapters.

To the Revd F. Roger Tomes, M.A., B.D., my thanks for not just correcting my lay preaching, college and university Old Testament exercises years ago, but for willingly agreeing to do the same with this over-sized essay. If any errors have crept through it will be through the student's insistence that he thinks he knows better than his tutor!

Thanks also go to the Revd G. Roy Chapman, a former General Secretary of the International Bible Reading Association, for bringing his expertise into this book in so many different ways.

I would also thank Steve Ashton and the Continuing Education Department of Lancaster University for giving me confidence to step 'out of my depth' in going into print, through tuition in writing non-fiction, and to Elspeth Taylor, Senior Commissioning Editor of HarperCollins*Religious*, for putting me right when I have stepped outside the bounds of this area of tuition.

I began this book with a jest. I'll end it the same way. With tongue in cheek, I naturally totally deny the fact that having a B.Ed. [Hons] degree, and thus a potential to correct some of my grammatical errors, made Brenda, my bride of one year, even more attractive to this lonely author! Thanks for your patience and attempted explanations of how the English language works, B.

This is not an Oscar thanksgiving ceremony, so I won't show appreciation of every author of books that have influenced me over twenty-five years of preaching, nor of every tutor who has guided and helped. But to all who have had such patience over the years, I pray that this book, with all its limitations, may at least be a partial sign of appreciation.

RJG